BREAKING

TRAUMA IN THE NEWSROOM

Edited by
Leona O'Neill and Chris Lindsay

Breaking: Trauma in the Newsroom
First published in 2022 by Maverick House Publishers,
Unit 33, The Business Centre, Stadium Business Park,
Ballycoolin, Dublin 11, Ireland.

Web: www.maverickhouse.com
Email: info@maverickhouse.com
@maverick_house

Print ISBN: 978-1-908518-69-9
ePub ISBN: 978-1-908518-70-5

Dedication

This book is dedicated to Brendan and our children, who lit my path in the darkness, and to Emmet who reminded me that there was still good in the world.

Leona O'Neill

This book is dedicated to the memory of Tony Roscoe and Michael Brett, for their courage, to Catherine for her unerring love, kindness and support, and to Enid, for the sheer joy she brings, always.

Chris Lindsay

A note from the editors

We are both journalists who have been affected by witnessing acts of terrible violence through our work. One of us standing close to a young woman when she was shot dead by a gunman during a riot; the other injured in a bomb attack which almost claimed the life of a young man he was standing beside.

Those were both events one would naturally associate with the Troubles – although both happened after the Good Friday Agreement brought a semblance of peace to Northern Ireland. But we feel it is important to stress this is not a book solely about that conflict, although it does feature in its pages.

There are also stories here from reporters, camera operators and photographers who had to process trauma because of their jobs unrelated to the violence they witnessed on the streets of Northern Ireland. There are stories of how exposure to seemingly endless deaths in a London hospital ward during the Covid pandemic, reporting on the brutal murder of a woman on her honeymoon in Mauritius, the drowning of a family in an Irish seaside resort, or covering the carnage of the war in Iraq left marks on those members of the media. They have seen and heard things which cannot be unseen, or unheard. Some have suffered Post Traumatic Stress Disorder (PTSD) as a consequence while others have had to cope with other psychiatric and psychological challenges. Some have had to leave their jobs. The impact of trauma is the common thread that runs through this book.

We hope that the courage they have shown in contributing their stories, and revealing their scars, will feed into a wider conversation about how those who work in the media are supported in terms of their mental health. We think that is a critical conversation, and one that needs to include those who are training to work in journalism, and those conducting that training. We would like to offer our profound gratitude to those who have told their stories in this book.

Leona O'Neill and Chris Lindsay

Foreword by Denis Murray OBE

Reporters witness – they see, hear, and least remarked on, smell things that are not part of what might be described as the common experience. In my own career, spent almost entirely in Ireland and the UK, I can tell you how long a young healthy male can survive without food; how long someone can scream on hearing of the death of a loved one; what burning human flesh smells like; how hot a petrol bomb is at the point of impact; and differentiate between the sounds made by a pistol and a high velocity rifle.

I can also differentiate between the sounds made by a blast bomb and a firework. Fireworks (rockets, bangers and so on) became part of riots in the late 1990s and early 2000s, as they were legalised and became readily available for purchase. I hate the damn things. They are noisy and dangerous. But the bang they make, you come to realise, is just a bang. Blast bombs rip the air – they're not just louder, there's a different quality to the sound. It's as if Shakespeare's tear in the fabric of the natural order has happened.

And so the chapter in this book by my old BBC colleague Chris Lindsay is the one with which I am most familiar. I was there. Only not right beside him, but on the opposite side of the Crumlin Road in north Belfast. At about the same time as he was wounded by a blast bomb, my cameraman, producer and I were being hit by a police water cannon, which may I tell you is a deeply unpleasant experience (if not on the same scale as brushing with death and explosives).

All that said, we signed up for this, we volunteered to go to places where there was likely, probably or definitely going to be at least the unpleasant, and at worst, the downright dangerous. Once a BBC presenter said to me live on air "this must be a very difficult story to cover", which it was, but which was most definitely not the point. If you were upset by something – which everybody who covered the Troubles was, at least on occasion – you got upset in private.

Nobody in Northern Ireland journalism was prepared for the Troubles. My generation, starting in the mid 1970s, knew what it was in for; and there was the newly-won experience and advice of the by-now old hands on which to rely.

For some of us it was a single incident; for some it was the sheer longevity of the conflict that got to us. And some of us sailed (or appeared to sail) quite unperturbed through the whole thing. This applies across the board. Jeremy Bowen of the BBC some years ago did a documentary about war reporters, all of whom had problems of one sort or other – he and Fergal Keane have both said publicly that they suffer from PTSD. But the weird thing for Northern Irish journalists in particular is that we were witnessing and reporting on conflict in our own streets and fields. It was personal.

I don't want to exaggerate all this – you could certainly say that police, fire, ambulance, hospital staff, the social workers who picked up the pieces, had far worse experiences than the journos did. You could also say that anyone who lived in the most conflicted parts of Northern Ireland would have shared precisely the knowledge and experience outlined in my second paragraph. But, oddly, what bothered me a great deal was that all the emergency and other services were actually doing something – all I was doing was telling people's stories. And it took me a while to realise that is something really good and important too because, at its heart, journalism is about people.

In this book journalists tell their own stories. Which will go against the grain – journalists love telling stories, and anecdotes, but they do not like talking about themselves.

Relish these stories – journalists are your eyes and ears. And they are your voice too – it's important to hear theirs.

Denis Murray OBE

Contents

Contents

Hard Cover

Chris Lindsay

CHRIS LINDSAY has been a BBC staff journalist since 1999. He was Network Producer on the BBC's Ireland Bureau for more than a decade, covering stories for UK and global outlets. He has also worked as a senior broadcast journalist for BBC Northern Ireland's TV News, Politics and Radio Current Affairs departments.

Ardoyne, north Belfast, 12 July 2005: "I'm dying, I'm going to fucking die, please God tell my Mum and Dad I love them!" screamed the young man gripping my hand in the back of the ambulance. Blood was pumping out of a gaping leg wound, covering the floor.

"You're not going to fucking die, fucking stay with me!" barked a burly paramedic as he struggled to clamp a huge compress on this shattered leg. My hands were covered with my own blood from a shrapnel wound inflicted by a similar device minutes earlier.

I had wanted to be a journalist for as long as I could remember and my obsession was the Troubles. Bombings, shootings and riots had darkly fascinated me since I was a kid. I started out as a trainee reporter for my local paper, the *Antrim Guardian*, in the mid 90s. By the summer of 1996, after making the jump to Belfast to try my hand as a freelancer, I was also working for one of the major taxi companies on the dispatch desk. At the time, the taxi drivers' radio was a critical source of news. Taxi drivers were often first to hear about a bomb scare or a riot. So many of them were murdered, they did their best to keep their colleagues informed and safe from danger. When there was trouble on the streets, like Drumcree 1996 after the blocking of an Orange march in Portadown led to serious rioting across Northern Ireland, there were clashes at virtually every interface in Belfast. The taxi tannoy would crackle with warnings about civil disorder, reports of gunmen on the streets, and burning vehicles blocking roads.

Every time I heard a new piece of info, I'd slip outside to the phone box with a handful of ten pence coins and ring all the news desks with tip offs. That's how I made my name in Belfast and moved on to getting bylines in the daily newspapers before a stint in commercial radio. By 1998 I was in the BBC newsroom, populated with some of the best and best-known journalists in the United Kingdom.

The first riot I covered for the BBC was in the wake of solicitor Rosemary Nelson's murder in March 1999. She was killed in Lurgan by an under-car booby trap bomb attack by loyalist paramilitaries. I was on the Good Morning Ulster radio programme late shift and we were picking up reports of serious violence on the Garvaghy Road in Portadown. Nelson had worked for a nationalist residents' group there who opposed Orange Order marches passing their homes. I travelled in the crew car to the riot with one of the BBC's TV reporters, Yvette Shapiro. As the petrol bombs rained down and the plastic baton rounds cracked across the tarmac, she helped me keep as safe as possible. At one stage an officer in riot gear shouted, "hard cover!" Yvette grabbed me, pulling me behind a Land Rover.

"If you hear 'hard cover', that means the cops or army think they've seen a gunman," she told me as we crouched beside the vehicle. "You get behind the wheel arch of a car and keep down."

I'd covered trouble on the streets before, but this was different: I was a BBC journalist now, and I had to get as close to the action as possible to get the best audio for my report for Good Morning Ulster. I was simultaneously frightened and exhilarated: I wanted to prove myself, and I desperately wanted to have the lead story on the programme.

The rioting tapered off by 2am and I stayed up until 6am cutting a package. It made the lead. I didn't sleep at all that day, buzzing on the high of the night before. My reporting from the Garvaghy Road taught me a lot about covering violence on the streets. Listen to experienced colleagues. Know that you're going to be scared. Accept that you're going to be high on adrenaline because you want the best audio and the best pictures. Understand that part of you is becoming hooked on the high that being immersed in the action brings.

The dispute over the Holy Cross Primary School blockade was the first time I found myself covering serious violence sustained over the course of several weeks. I was working as a producer for the BBC's Network News Ireland Bureau. I was part of a team competing against Sky, ITN, Al Jazeera and many other media outlets from around the world, at a time when a story from Northern Ireland again became international news. Only 9/11 ended the global focus on the Holy Cross situation.

As far back as June 2001, when loyalists blocked Catholic primary schoolgirls from making their way to school up the Ardoyne Road in North Belfast, there was night after night of rioting with petrol bombs, blast bombs and gunmen on the streets from both sides, at the flashpoint with Ardoyne, and at other sectarian interfaces. When the new school term started, loyalists again blockaded the road leading to the school. Police used their batons to drive them into side streets. The standoff went on for several days, and every morning the BBC Network team would walk up with the schoolgirls. One morning, things dramatically escalated: loyalists rolled a blast bomb at police and troops as they protected the children and their parents. There was pandemonium – little girls running and screaming, loyalists clashing with police and army in a side street, and a police officer rolling on the ground in agony after being hit by shrapnel from that explosive device. Fast-forward to 2005, and 500 yards down the road, I was to witness at much closer quarters the savage damage to flesh and bone these improvised grenades could cause.

For several years, republican groups in Ardoyne had tried to stop Orangemen and their supporters from passing shops off the Crumlin Road on their return to Ligoniel during their annual 12 July march. In 2004, rioting had erupted after the police cleared the road to allow the loyalists through. It was vicious, but not prolonged. But 2005 was to be different.

I arrived on the Ardoyne Road with my colleagues: Ireland Correspondents Denis Murray and Kevin Connolly, cameraman Peter Cooper, and Bureau Chief Kevin Kelly. The Orange Order march was still a couple of hours away, and as we walked down the Ardoyne Road, the air was thick with the smell of petrol. I encountered some well-known members of the Provisional IRA, pouring the contents of a crate of petrol bombs they'd uncovered down a drain.

"What's it looking like tonight, lads?" I asked.

"What do you think?" replied one of the men emptying bottles full of petrol. "Not too fucking good is what I think it's looking like."

It was clear that the Provisionals did not want rioting in the area on this occasion and had not come to fight. It was also clear, however, that dissident republicans opposed to the peace process were planning serious trouble.

Over the course of several years, I stood at the roundabout at Ardoyne, waiting for the Orangemen to return from the biggest day in the marching season. The tension was always palpable; the waiting always was the worst part. There would be huge numbers of riot police, often with military support, large crowds of republicans held back at the top of the Crumlin Road, and loyalists behind security barricades at Twaddell Avenue waiting to cheer on the marchers. Then you'd hear it in the distance – the sound of the bands accompanying the Orangemen as they made their way up the Crumlin Road, the growing jeers from the republican side, the responding cheers from the loyalists, and the ever-present percussive buzz of army and police helicopters watching from above.

In 2005, as the marchers passed, republicans threw missiles over police lines at the Orangemen, and Orange stewards hurriedly pushed the marchers up the road, trying to avoid the incoming projectiles. When the Orangemen had passed the shops, the serious trouble began. Republican youths pelted the security forces with masonry, bottles, and petrol bombs, and a car was set on fire. The police pushed their Land Rovers into the middle of the Ardoyne roundabout and deployed a water cannon. The bombardment of missiles from the republican side was unrelenting. I'd positioned myself with most other members of the press pack behind the police vehicles.

There's nowhere safe in a serious riot but behind police lines is where journalists tend to gather. That's where I found myself, just in front of Ardoyne Ambulance depot, with the rioting becoming more intense on the other side of the police line – bellicose, angry masked youths were hurling more petrol bombs at the police, daring them to come out of their armoured vehicles and fight: flinging bricks, masonry, bottles: anything they could get their hands on. Suddenly there was a huge bang at the roundabout, behind police lines. The press pack collectively flinched.

I was holding my minidisc microphone to capture audio. I still have the recording of what happened next – a police officer shouts "get back!". I look up, and see something rolling towards me: a length of copper piping, with nails and bolts strapped round it with masking tape, and a fuse viciously fizzing. Everything slows down. I know what this is. It's a blast bomb packed with shrapnel. I turn ninety degrees, and make it two steps away before it detonates with a savage, concussive boom. I feel searing pain in my back.

Then there's another explosion. I'm running, and I put my hand to where the pain is. It comes back covered in blood. I have been wounded, I don't know how badly I am hurt, I am falling down onto the pavement, I am hyperventilating, I am terrified, and then the police are trying to drag me to an ambulance. They make one attempt and have to pull back as another blast bomb comes in.

I can hear an officer shouting over his radio, I assume to his commander, "This is a fucking life-threatening situation!" Then they make another attempt to drag me into an ambulance. I'm deaf and I'm in shock. I'm pushed in and a young man is lying on a stretcher, writhing in agony: he's ashen and he's clearly been terribly injured. There's blood everywhere. He grabs my hand. He screams that he thinks he is dying. He begs me to tell his mother and father he loves them. His nails dig into my bloody hands. He is Simon Taylor, and one of the blast bombs used in this Continuity IRA attack, launched from the top of nearby shops, has torn his leg to pieces. Simon Taylor is now 43 years old and works in London. This is the first time we have spoken since we were in that ambulance.

"I saw it hit the pavement beside me at the roundabout, and I knew, in a millisecond, that it was a blast bomb. I turned, and thankfully I turned the right way, because if I'd turned the other way, I'd have been killed," he recalled.

"I thought I'd sprained my ankle and I dragged myself to police lines and fell to the ground. They formed a protective shell over me, and I could hear them shouting 'We have to get him out!' – and the reply: 'We can't get him out, there's still incoming'.

The police and paramedics did eventually get him into the back of an ambulance.

"I remember being cold. The pain was extraordinary. I could smell my own burnt flesh. My bones had been powdered. I can remember the ambulance being hit with a hell of a lot of bricks. I was thinking 'Are they even trying to get me in the ambulance?' One of the last memories of that evening is at the Mater Hospital, the medics were rapidly cutting my clothes away, and it was just like...a bloodbath. Then I was taken to theatre, it was the first of seven operations. The first op took seven hours," he said.

"My girlfriend (now wife) went to the chapel at the Mater and prayed because it looked like I might not make it. The next day it was touch and go. I'd lost so much blood they were giving me more and more transfusions. Later I was shown X-rays and it looked like someone had blasted half of B&Q into me – washers, bolts and nails had just shredded my flesh, femur, and pelvis. I had to have several skin grafts.

"I lost an inch and a half off my left leg and 15 years on I need more surgery. I'm still startled by sudden loud noises."

Simon says those riot police who risked their safety getting him into the ambulance while the Continuity IRA ambush continued, and that paramedic who wrestled the compress onto his appalling wound – Michael Brett – saved his life.

Brett had himself experienced terrible tragedy as the result of terrorism, three years after the Good Friday Agreement was supposed to have ushered in a new era of peace in Northern Ireland: his 18-year-old son Gavin was shot dead in a random sectarian shooting in 2001 by loyalist paramilitaries the UFF, close to the family home. Michael tried in vain to save his son's life. He died in his arms.

"When I heard Mr Brett had passed away in 2007, that hit me," Simon told me. "He'd come to visit me in the days after the explosion at Ardoyne. He worked on saving people's lives despite his own dreadful loss. He was a decent, brave man."

Brett was indeed a true hero. Our encounter was brief, and took place in the midst of bloody chaos. Had Michael been in the military, he would have been awarded a medal for gallantry for his actions that night. He put himself in harm's way to save the life of someone who would almost certainly otherwise have died on the street. He pulled on a helmet and had Taylor stretchered into the ambulance, while blast bombs, bricks and petrol bombs rained down. How he managed to continue after all he had endured with the murder of "my big son", as he called him, in his arms, I simply cannot imagine. But because of his actions, another young man lived to have his own son. A hero.

I was relatively lucky that night. Fortunately, I had been wearing a backpack filled with body armour and other protective gear that took the brunt of the blast bomb that injured me. The bottom of that backpack was smoking and shredded. It could have been my spine. I sustained a flesh wound from a small red-hot shard, but because I made it that critical step away, there was no organ damage. I saw the bomb with its fizzing fuse rolling towards me, so I was able to turn and wasn't blinded, or worse. I had a shard of shrapnel pulled out of my back.

As I was carried in, the waiting area was a scene of mayhem, full of police: around 100 officers were injured that night. Some of those were waiting for treatment, some there to protect their colleagues from any further attack. A journalist from a national newspaper was clutching a bandaged hand: a police dog had bitten him when the riot squad moved down the Crumlin Road, in the same manoeuvre which saw Denis Murray and Gerry Adams blasted with a water cannon. Murray and the rest of my team were on the far side of police lines from where Simon and I had been injured. Denis' memories of that night remain vivid.

"In a career of around 40 years, it's the only time I saw so many journalists injured, hit in one way or another," Denis told me.

"After the parade had passed, relatively peacefully, when I was honestly just thinking 'that one wasn't too bad', suddenly everything went absolutely crazy. We were facing a phalanx of security force vehicles head on, so I couldn't actually see where Chris was, he was only about 100 yards away but he might as well have been on the dark side of the moon.

"I was standing with cameraman Peter Cooper and our producer Kevin Kelly, with our backs to the wall of the shops on the Crumlin Road. At this stage, the parade having passed, the police would usually have cleared off. But a double line of riot police came sweeping down with dogs and pushed anyone who got in their way, which included every journalist, in front of their lines. The police were clearly terrified. I had seen many riots before, but these were young, fresh recruits and they did not want to be there. The crowd went absolutely crazy and a pitched battle began.

"They turned on the water cannon and I saw the jet coming and had a second to turn my head away before it hit. It's a horrible sensation – like drowning in air. The same water cannon also hit the local parish priest Father Aidan Troy and then Sinn Fein leader Gerry Adams.

"Peter Cooper and Kevin Kelly's heads clashed in the melee, and blood started pouring from Peter's nose. People came out of a small corner shop with kitchen roll and helped him to staunch the bleeding. My fellow correspondent Kevin Connolly was hit by a brick thrown by the rioters.

"Then we could hear revving and a car that was clearly put aside for this purpose came roaring around the corner, two young fellas jumped out and petrol bombed it, so you then had this car blazing.

"At this point we felt we'd filmed all we usefully could and still be able to edit a report for the Ten O'Clock News, and managed to get back into the crew car. That's when Kelly got a call to say that Chris had been hit with shrapnel from a blast bomb. Much later that evening Chris came stumbling into the newsroom and he was white and shaking and I said 'Are you OK?' and he said 'Apart from this thing in my back, I think I'm OK.'

I said 'come on now, I feel like shit and I've only been hit with the water cannon, I feel terrible, are you OK?' He showed me this huge dressing on the small of his back, and his white shirt was drenched in blood. But he just tried to brush it off.

"So that was a night when five people from the one team all got hit in separate locations and there but for the Grace of God, Chris would have been very seriously injured. When

Lyra McKee was killed 14 years later at a riot in Derry, after a gunman fired at police lines, Peter Cooper and I, who were both retired at this stage, had a conversation. We both said, "can you remember the number of nights you stood with the police and a republican or a loyalist fired shots at the police lines and nobody was so much as scratched?" It came home to both of us, and we regard ourselves as fairly gnarly, brass-necked old hacks, it made us think and reminded us of how shaken we were by that night in Ardoyne.

It was a night when the only way to avoid what happened was not to be there. I was much more shocked by the events of that night in the days that followed than I was on the night. I learned the lesson that it's not just what happens that day: it's what happens when you feel dizzy the next day, and when you have to say, "I'm not going to the next riot and here's why".

Two days after the riot, a colleague stopped me and asked if I was OK. I told him I was grand, I was lucky, I was fine. He looked at me with concern and said: "God, Chris, if that had been a coffee jar bomb with two pounds of Semtex in it, they'd have been scraping you off the road."

He wasn't being malicious or trying to upset me, but suddenly my world tilted on its axis: I felt faint and a sense of dislocation from reality. I was dizzy and the strength went from my legs. I had to sit down. I'd been high on adrenaline and alcohol for 48 hours and suddenly I crashed. What if the Continuity IRA had access to the sort of explosives the Provisional IRA had used with such deadly effect? He was right. They didn't, and it hadn't happened – but what if, my thoughts churned insistently: what if? What would have been left to scrape off the road?

The days and weeks after the ambush were tough. Images and thoughts repeatedly played themselves over and over in my mind – the blast bomb rolling towards me; the knowledge I'd been hit; the uncertainty over how badly I'd been hurt; the screams from Taylor in the ambulance as it careered and jolted over rubble on the Crumlin Road on its way to the Mater Hospital as he gripped my hand.

I was subject to violent mood swings. One minute I'd be rushing on the adrenaline of what I'd been through and escaped relatively unscathed from, the next the constant 'what-ifs' would return. What if I hadn't seen the bomb? What if I hadn't been wearing my backpack full of protective gear?

My temper was short, and for a while I drank a lot more than usual. I was diagnosed by a clinical psychiatrist as having an adjustment disorder, a condition that occurs when a person has difficulty coping with, or adjusting to, a particular source of stress, such as a major life change, loss, or event.

I was well looked after by the BBC. Before the chaos of that night in Ardoyne, they had trained me to deal with hostile environments. After my injury, they offered me counselling. They also offered me time off. They told me I didn't have to go out and cover rioting again if I didn't feel up to it.

For a few months, I admit I couldn't. When there was wide-spread rioting in Belfast later that summer, I stayed at my desk trying to co-ordinate the BBC Network response. But, a year later, by 12 July 2006, I felt I had to push myself, and part of me wanted that rush again. I was back.

In December 2012, the loyalist flag protests erupted after Belfast City Council ruled to restrict when the Union Flag could be flown at City Hall. Gangs of protestors set up road-blocks all over the city and there was rioting in many loyalist areas in Belfast and beyond. Working for BBC Network News, we were like a flying column for trouble spots. Northern Ireland was again an international story, and we needed the best pictures. They would flash around the world and again we were in competition with teams from rival broadcasters from across the globe as they arrived in Belfast.

A difficult truth about being a local journalist on the frontline, when Northern Ireland on occasion descends into chaos, is that while you may have insider knowledge, you also have an undeniable lack of distance from the situation. Belfast is a small city and events overlap and intersect with eerie frequency.

During the flag protests, I covered serious rioting in loyalist areas of Belfast – places like The Village and Sandy Row in the south of the city and at flashpoints in the east, as well as in towns like Carrickfergus in County Antrim. One Friday night, I arrived with a camera crew at a roundabout on the sprawling Rathcoole estate on the fringes of north Belfast, where a large crowd had gathered to block roads, and tried to set up in a safe location. We were immediately the deliberate target of a fusillade of petrol bombs and had to beat a hasty retreat to a distance beyond their reach.

Life turns and overlaps in strange cycles in a society as small as Northern Ireland: my paternal grandparents, like so many others in the early years of the Troubles, were forced out of their homes. They lost everything from their tiny terrace house in the mainly Catholic Ardoyne and were moved to the Prot-estant Rathcoole estate with literally only the clothes on their backs – into the third storey of a bleak block of flats with no lift. Both had chronic bronchial problems. My grandmother was in and out of psychiatric units for the rest of her life. Having been injured by republican paramilitaries in Ardoyne, I then became the target of loyalists hurling petrol and blast bombs with the same intent in Rathcoole – an area my team were only able to go into because I knew every street and alleyway in that urban maze. I knew how to get in, and, more importantly, how to get out.

That night in Rathcoole at the Cloughfern roundabout, we captured the scene as a distraught man tried to visit his wife in a nearby nursing home but couldn't get past the loyalist road-block. As he pleaded to be let through, he was in tears, and was met with jeers from protestors – some even chanted 'Cheerio, cheerio, cheerio!'. When we were spotted filming him, loyal-ists targeted us again with bricks, bottles and petrol bombs. We had it in the can, so we headed back to base to edit our TV and radio packages. For me, this seemingly small moment amidst months of rioting, roadblocks and protests, was a singularly harrowing experience. My mother had died two years previously in the same nursing home, a victim of early onset Alzheimer's. I saw in this man my late father, who stayed with her for three cruel years, feeding her every meal, until she finally passed away. Another overlap. Another coincidence.

In January 2013, the flag protests were relentless and after that riot in Rathcoole, the next day I was back on the street – as thousands of loyalists had descended on Belfast city centre for a rally. As they tried to return to east Belfast, whatever agreement had been reached with the police unravelled (recol-lections differ on both sides) and serious violence erupted on the Albertbridge Road. That Saturday afternoon, I was producer and backwatcher (the eyes and ears of a cameraman who can only see what's in their lens) for one of the best I've worked with – the late Tony Roscoe.

Tony captured the iconic pictures of nationalists and loyalists engaged in hand-to-hand fighting on the Albertbridge Road, then rioting which continued for ten long hours as the police pushed a loyalist crowd past the nationalist Short Strand enclave and deeper into east Belfast. That's the one day I remember most acutely rushing on the high when fear and adrenaline combine in equal measure. A burning car's petrol tank blew seconds after we ran past. I was hit by golf balls and bricks; Tony had a laser pen aimed right down his lens and needed treatment to his eye. I got away with minor bruising. Then in the early hours of Sunday morning, the last brick was thrown, the last petrol bomb hurled. It was time to try and unwind and process everything I'd absorbed. I fell asleep at around 7am and slept until 7pm. Then, the phone buzzed: more loyalist roadblocks had been set up in east Belfast: one at the Short Strand flashpoint, and riot police had moved in to keep rival factions apart. By 8pm, I was there with my crew.

All of the eruptions of violence I've reported on for the BBC happened when Northern Ireland was regarded by the outside world as being at peace. All of them happened after the Good Friday Agreement was signed in 1998. I don't regard Northern Ireland as having secured full peace – the period since that agreement was signed has not been marked by significant reconciliation between the two communities, and there have been sporadic outbreaks of sometimes very severe violence. I hope I am wrong, but I fear it is unlikely that Northern Ireland has seen its last riot.

The way news organisations gather pictures during disturbances has changed immeasurably since I was putting those ten pence pieces into a phone box to give newsrooms tip offs. It's now more likely than not that the first pictures will be captured not by the BBC, or ITN, or Sky – but by members of the public on their camera phones.

News organisations will scramble to get pictures of their own, but we also now have to sift through what can be large quantities of material taken by bystanders, or those involved in the incident. In that respect, the game has changed. When we deploy, we make sure it's people who are experienced and equipped with the right safety gear.

The blast bomb attack that injured me was 17 years ago. Understanding and support for mental health has become much more advanced since then and support is certainly more widely available. If you're in the game and need it, ask. Whether or not serious rioting returns to the streets of Northern Ireland, the journalists of the future need to know that they're going to require real psychological and emotional resilience, because even if it isn't a riot or other potentially dangerous event, by the very nature of our jobs we are exposed to and absorb a lot of trauma: murders, road accidents, various people's personal tragedies, bereavements, disturbing evidence in court – especially when covering crimes of violence or sexual assault. That stuff can take its toll as well.

One of the most distressing experiences I had in 25 years of journalism didn't take place on the streets. It was in Omagh Courthouse, at an inquest. The 999 call of a young girl who died with her four siblings and mother, in a house fire deliberately started by her stepfather, was played to the court.

"Help me...I'm burning...run!" she screamed, as flames consumed the house. Towards the end of the recording, we heard what's believed to be her last, agonizing breaths. I can still hear that call. It haunts me. And I know I am not alone.

My advice to young journalists embarking on their careers would be to avail of every single bit of training they can get. I've given talks to journalism classes on how to cover riots as safely as possible. Seek out courses that deal with how you can build your resilience and be as ready as you can be if you run into danger. Listen to experienced colleagues and tutors, because they can be an invaluable source of support and advice. Covering riots and civil disorder is always going to have an element of danger. But you can do your best to stack the odds in your favour.

My days of having the overwhelming urge to be first out the door when trouble kicks off, grabbing a rucksack full of safety gear and jumping into the car with a crew are gone. The birth of my daughter had an impact on how I felt. It wasn't just my safety to consider any more. Did I want my child to see her father harmed because he was gung-ho to get yet more pictures, more audio, ever closer to the action, when I'd done it for over a decade? No. Not worth it. Been there, done that, got the bloody shirt.

No peace for me on these streets

Leona O'Neill

LEONA O'NEILL is a Lecturer in Journalism at Ulster University. She has worked for the *Belfast Telegraph*, the *Irish News* and other newspapers throughout Northern Ireland as well as being a field producer for a number of international news agencies.

"I often woke up screaming, shouting or gasping for breath."

I hadn't noticed the sun coming up behind the houses on our street, the darkness suddenly lifting surprised me. I had been sitting in my car outside my house for several hours. I was shaking as the mixture of cold and adrenaline that had enabled me to walk back to my car in Creggan and drive home wore off. I couldn't go into my house because I feared the emotional barrier that I always used to distance myself from the horrors of the job would come crashing down when I looked at my husband and kids. I didn't want to see them sleeping, thinking it was a sight I might never have seen again had one of those bullets, fired towards police vehicles and that I could hear whistling past my ear as I ran, hit me.

As I sat there in the dawn light, the police tweeted out confirmation of what all of us standing on that cold Creggan street in Derry had feared. Lyra McKee had died. Still numb, I retweeted their message, and said that I was standing beside this young woman when she fell and that I felt sick to my stomach. My phone immediately started ringing. It was reporters from radio and television stations I had worked with across the world wanting me to relay what I had seen. I couldn't get what I had just seen out of my head. I could still smell the smoke from the burning vehicles off my clothes. On autopilot, I said the same five sentences almost word for word to 50 different stations, to strangers and colleagues alike.

"I heard the shots and I ran for cover. She was just laying there on the ground, we didn't know what had hit her. My friend put his coat under her head and I phoned an ambulance. The police put her in the back of their vehicle and crashed through the burning barricades. They took her to hospital where she tragically died."

I was glad to stay in reporter mode, it meant that I didn't have to go into my house and see the framed picture memories on the wall that might have been all I left my family with. There was no comfort for me in my car, and that was OK with me.

My husband came out of the house asking me to come in, to do the interviews where it was warm. He said he'd make me tea. Was I alright? I couldn't even look at him, I couldn't bear anyone being nice to me, because I might break into a million pieces if that barrier fell.

I couldn't sit in my home with the smiling and innocent eyes of my children looking down from the frames on the walls and think or speak about murder and hatred and guns and people taking their last breaths on the cold ground. My home was my safe haven. I couldn't shatter that peace with such brutal words. So I sat where I was, in the cold car, my head spinning, my heart racing and my stomach churning. I couldn't bear to be in a warm house, safe with my family around me when there was a poor, innocent woman lying dead in the hospital who would never see her family again.

I needed to stay in professional, stoic mode to survive. I needed not to think, just to carry on. That was the safest thing to do. I sat there all night and well into the morning. Call after call after call. Yes, I'll do it. Yes, live in 10 seconds, OK. The same story over and over and over again. I was in shock. I felt like a robot, like my brain and my mouth were totally unconnected, that I was distant and disconnected from life somehow. I spoke to strangers with English, American, Australian accents.

After nine o'clock a friend called. A fellow journalist.

"Are you alright?" he asked. In all the conversations throughout the night, no one had asked that particular question, they just wanted the details of what had happened. My brain could barely compute what he was saying but his voice was familiar and felt like home after speaking all night to journalists from across the world. It unexpectedly grounded me. I felt warm tears roll down my freezing cold face.

"I dunno," I said. And I didn't. I honestly didn't. My ability to function, to think, to feel anything had disappeared. I was just numb.

Less than 12 hours earlier I had been at an election hustings event in Derry city centre when my cameraman friend called and told me that there seemed to be a security alert in Creggan. He was off work that night but saw at least 12 police vehicles drive past him, including army bomb disposal units.

Creggan is a huge, sprawling working class housing estate on a hill overlooking Derry's ancient walled city. It is a place where perfectly kept council houses and small, proudly maintained gardens sit in stark contrast with the murals of masked gun-wielding IRA volunteers on gable walls and graffiti championing violent dissident republicans is roughly scrawled on shop shutters.

Tensions were already high in the estate that Easter Thursday night because a planned dissident republican commemoration was due to take place on Monday. It was an illegal parade, the police said that they would enforce the law and dissidents said they would oppose the restrictions.

Exactly a year earlier I had been on the same Creggan streets when serious rioting broke out as masked youths petrol bombed a path for marchers in paramilitary garb in the same commemoration. Trouble was expected this year again and tensions had already spilled over with attacks on police vehicles in Creggan during the days leading up to Lyra's death.

Myself and my best friend Emmet arrived at the scene of what we thought was a bomb alert shortly after 9pm. I was working for Q Radio and the *Belfast Telegraph*. I began populating my social media platforms with videos of forensics officers examining a house in a residential street, Mulroy Gardens.

There was a huge security presence in the area. Both sides of the street were filled with back-to-back police vehicles and the bomb squad. No one seemed to know what was going on, but a crowd of youths had gathered and the atmosphere was getting increasingly hostile.

There is a strange relationship between police and public in most nationalist and republican areas in Northern Ireland. Police are generally not welcomed, particularly by youths, who show their displeasure with bricks and bottles.

In Mulroy Gardens people were shouting at the police and residents were getting increasingly angry. There was nowhere that provided shelter or cover and I felt exposed and uncomfortable.

I heard glass smashing on the next street over – Fanad Drive – and walked through an alleyway to see two police vehicles being pelted with bricks and bottles by youths who had gathered at a junction. I got myself into a safe position behind a wall and filmed some footage of rioting that over the next two hours got consistently worse.

I work with many international TV crews who are often quite bewildered by the Northern Ireland 'style' of rioting. These riots are more often than not, contained within residential areas and happen practically on people's doorsteps. Often life goes on as normal as they rage on and the streets are in flames.

That night as, at the bottom of the street, youths pelted the police vehicles with petrol bombs and fireworks lit up the night sky like we were at some weird festival, I walked around speaking with people who had been standing at their front doors watching what was happening. Women stood with babies on their hips chatting at their gates as the streets burned. Teenagers walked past on their way to meet their friends, taking selfies in the middle of the road. People were laughing and chatting and just watching things unfold.

A little girl spoke to me. She was around eight years old, the same age as my own daughter. She said she was making her First Communion soon and wanted to tell me about her dress. Thinking of my own precious girl safe back at home, I said her dress sounded absolutely beautiful but that she should go home because her Mum would be so worried if she had heard there was rioting and she wasn't home and safe.

I remember a loud cheer going up in the crowd which had gathered at the junction – mostly young people standing observing – and seeing two hijacked vehicles being positioned at the crossroads. They were set alight and, having frequented many riots over the years, I knew there would probably have been firearms involved in the hijacking and that the petrol tanks wouldn't be long exploding, so I moved further up the street again to what I perceived was relative 'safety'.

Fireworks were being constantly shot at the police vehicles, lighting up the night and the faces of those, young and old, lining the street.

Just after 11pm as I was leaning up against a wall filing my story from my phone I heard the distinctive crack of gunfire. I knew immediately it was not fireworks and I ducked and as more shots rang out I ran up the street and behind another wall for cover, shouting as I went "it's shots, get down!". As I ran I could hear the bullets whizzing and whistling past my head.

Hardly anyone on the street moved.

"It's just fireworks," a man shouted at me, "wise up!".

I felt foolish for a moment and second-guessed what I might have heard. From my position behind the wall I looked straight in front of me to what appeared at first glance to be a pile of clothes at the wheel of the police vehicle. Someone asked: "Where's Lyra?"

A woman beside me started screaming, a horrible, deep animalistic scream that haunted my nightmares for months afterwards. People rushed towards Lyra on the ground as the cracks and bangs continued. Total and utter panic ensued. No one knew what happened.

My friend Emmet took off his coat and put it under Lyra's head as she lay on the ground. A woman tending to her screamed for someone to call an ambulance. I dialled 999. I could barely string a sentence together.

"I need an ambulance...someone's been hurt. I don't know what happened. I don't know. I think she's been hit with some-thing. I don't know if she's still breathing, I can't get near her to check her pulse, she's on the ground and there's a crowd around her now...Is she still breathing? Please someone check her pulse, the paramedics need to know..."

All I could see was the poor girl's face. And it's all I've ever been able to see since.

There were screams for someone with a car to come and take her to hospital. There was talk of lifting her to the next street to get a car. People were crying, wailing, panicking, shouting. Some, who had just arrived on the scene, were screaming at the police vehicles that it was their fault – because of Lyra's small stature they had mistakenly thought that a young girl had been run over by one of their vehicles.

Emmet banged on the door of the police vehicle and an officer got out, saw Lyra lying on the ground and moved quickly to help her. A woman walked up with her mobile phone, filming, and I shouted at her to put it away. She ignored me and carried on. I tried to explain to the ambulance crew that they might not be able to get into our location as the street was blocked-off by barricades that were ablaze.

The smoke from the burning vehicles was choking, fireworks were still exploding, every bang I thought was more shots. A woman ran screaming down the street, screeching at the crowd gathered who had cheered as the gunman fired. No one standing over Lyra, at that precise chaotic, noisy, frantic moment in time knew if she had been shot or hit with a brick, a firework or if something else had felled her. None of us could see the bottom of the street so were unaware of a gunman firing towards us at that stage.

Lyra was lifted into the back of the police vehicle, a fact I relayed to the ambulance dispatcher before hanging up. The doors were slammed shut with a thud, they put on their sirens and sped down the road, crashing through the burning barricade and away to the hospital where she tragically died. It all happened in mere minutes. Seconds that changed so many people's lives.

As the sirens faded we were all left there in complete stunned silence. The fireworks had stopped. My friend Emmet stared at his hands, which were covered in blood. I looked down to the bottom of the street where the smoke still bellowed from the burning cars, the crowds still there.

No one spoke. There was nothing, absolutely nothing to say.

The next day I went to a peace vigil in the city centre. I was in deep shock, I hadn't slept. I couldn't even close my eyes. The feeling of numbness that descended over me as soon as the vehicle carrying Lyra sped off into the night had settled deep within me and I couldn't shake it off.

I had covered many riots and hostile environments over the years and I knew the dangers associated with them. Often, when the adrenaline wears off, you're left with the 'what ifs?' rattling around in your head. The gunman had fired four or five bullets. One of them hit Lyra. What if one of them had hit me? They were so close I could hear them whistling past my ears. And I had that particular 'what if' scenario played out in horrific and brutal detail in front of my very eyes the night before.

At the rally people came over and hugged me, asked me if I was OK. They were crying. I felt nothing at all except absolute pure undiluted horror, terror and a coldness that no matter how much time I spent in the shower that morning, would not wash away. My coat still smelled of smoke and the repulsion over what I had witnessed lingered just as heavily. I was in a daze.

I couldn't find the words to tell people about what I saw, so I went into robotic mode again. Yes, I'm doing alright. Yes, it is awful. Yes, poor Lyra. Awful, just awful. I was aware my words did absolutely no justice to the events of the previous night, but my mind couldn't even process what I had seen. I had terrible, terrible flashbacks and every time I closed my eyes I saw that poor girl's face. I saw her lying on the ground, curled around, almost hugging the police vehicle's wheel. But I felt I had to carry on, stay in reporter mode, that it would somehow protect me. I realise now that was not the best plan of action.

The *Belfast Telegraph* asked if I would write an account of what happened for the paper. I sat with my laptop open in a hotel cafe and for the first time in 20 years I just couldn't write. I didn't even know where to start. I couldn't formulate a sentence. My mind wouldn't cooperate. I couldn't put into words the gravity of the horror I had witnessed. There were no words to justify it. They wanted a colour piece, perhaps with emotion. What they got was the robotic relaying of the facts with little emotion, as cold as a police statement, because I simply wasn't capable of anything else. My brain had shut down, it had gone into preservation mode.

My Al Jazeera crew landed that afternoon to cover the story. I didn't know what I was doing, I just kept going. I greeted them as usual at the hotel lobby, our cameraman Chris and a reporter I hadn't met or worked with before. We travelled back up to the scene of the incident and I stood there looking at the place where Lyra had fallen and taken her last breaths just 18 hours previously. I was stunned, unable to form a thought process at all. People were saying words and I would watch their lips move as they spoke, but I didn't compute anything. My mind just wasn't working. Nothing felt real.

As our reporter interviewed some of Lyra's friends who were laying flowers I wondered when the numbness would wear off and whatever came next would hit me. I got through the next few days on absolute autopilot, so much so that when six months later I looked back on the news packages we had made about the shooting and despite spending three full days and nights with the reporter on the ground, I didn't even recognise him, remember him or any of the people we interviewed.

The staff at the *Belfast Telegraph* were so good. The editor and news editor called and asked if I was OK, that I could take time out, that they were behind me, anything I needed, just say. I said that I wanted to cover Lyra's funeral. I don't know why, I perhaps wanted closure. I perhaps wanted to show people I was still strong. That I was still the reporter I always was, that I was unbreakable.

I sat on the train from Derry and felt totally detached from everything and everyone around me. I still hadn't been able to sleep. I couldn't eat. I couldn't unravel from this heightened sense of panic. Everything felt so raw. I tried to ground myself by listening to music, but the surreal, numb feeling wouldn't subside.

I sat in the press pack at the funeral and could do nothing but stare at Lyra's coffin or divert my eyes to the devastation of her family. A singer performed You Dwell in My Soul so beautifully that I couldn't hold the tears back. I cried for the first time in days. In fact I sobbed. There in the press pack I was embarrassed by my emotion. I just felt it wasn't the done thing for reporters. I felt I needed to show I was strong, unmovable, hardnosed. Newsrooms are quite macho places where emotion is often seen as a weakness. I've had fellow journalists tell me that I shouldn't be moved by stories, not to make myself part of a story by showing emotions. Journalists are mere observers but I was completely torn between doing my job and being a human being who had seen this girl, this poor girl in a coffin before me, die on the street.

My journalist friend beside me asked if I was OK.

"Yep," I said, "I'm fine". Another lie. I was totally and utterly broken.

I hadn't been on social media much that week because everything felt so very raw and fragile and I didn't feel like talking to anyone or see pictures of Lyra. So when I logged back in I saw that I was being targeted by sick conspiracy theorists who, the day after Lyra's killing, made a vile video using all my footage from that night, claiming it was some kind of government conspiracy. They claimed that Lyra wasn't really dead and that I was complicit in covering up her disappearance and I should be hunted down. People discussed this in detail in comments, forums and social media then decided that because I had interviewed United States House Speaker Nancy Pelosi earlier that day, that I had somehow had Lyra killed as a sacrifice to her, to the illuminati or some other madness they had dreamt up to get hits on YouTube videos. They suggested I was involved in a false flag operation because I didn't film Lyra's death. I was tagged in countless comments and conversations on social media, all saying horrendous things.

"What kind of journalist is she that she didn't even film the most important part?" they screamed at me. I typed the words "I would never do that. I am a human being and I was calling a fucking ambulance at the time!" so many times and deleted it again. I just wasn't strong enough for the fight. I tried to ignore it, hoping it would go away. I couldn't believe that at my lowest ebb, people were attacking me, including people from my own city swept up in the hysteria. My lack of response just made things worse.

Over the next few weeks the abuse I received because of these mad theories was intense and relentless. They threatened to kill me "like I shot Lyra". They said they knew where I lived and were coming to burn my house down. I had hundreds upon hundreds of abusive comments and messages, some of them from people in my own city. My phone rang constantly and when I picked up no one would speak. People commented on social media that they wanted me to get cancer and die, people sent me screengrabs of forums where people said they were going to attack me on my way to work. They called for the police to arrest me. They threatened to hurt my children. People said they knew where I lived and worked and were going to stab me. Scores of strangers liked comments that threatened violence against me. Blogs were started that called me a liar, questioning if I had even been there that night or was just using the incident to further my career. The same was sprayed on a wall near where I worked. People said I was despicable and using the death of a colleague for my own means. People discussed how I was a thoroughly despicable human being.

I spoke to police about several local people who, from their relentless malicious and threatening messages, seemed to have serious mental health issues and made me very concerned for my safety. They lived in my city, seemed to know my routines and places I would frequent which made me nervous. One of them sent me a photo he had taken of me in a coffee shop. I was constantly looking over my shoulder, became hypervigilant and had a constant sense of unease. I was living in a constant, relentless, crushing state of fear.

Dissidents and their supporters didn't like the coverage of Lyra's killing and I was linked to that. Graffiti went up in my hometown saying that I wasn't welcome in certain areas and that I'd do "anything for a story". A woman in the street told me

I needed to "shut the fuck up about Lyra McKee". Later other
graffiti said that I was a 'tout', a claim that could be a death
sentence in Northern Ireland. I'd be shouted and screamed
at by big aggressive men in the street when covering stories.
There were countless threats against me.

Conspiracy theorist bloggers started fundraising appeals
to buy weapons to "wage war" on me. My credit cards were
hacked and money stolen from me. I was messaged by individuals warning me not to go to certain areas in my city or I
would be attacked, pulled out of my car and beaten up. They
told me I was "scum for using the death of a colleague to
further my career", asked me "how's your PTSD?", and if I
had killed myself yet. They mentioned places where I would
socialise. I knew these people knew me, knew where I lived,
where I worked. I worried that stories I was called to might be
a set up. For a while, every time I opened my messages there
was someone in there threatening me, my family or saying I
was an awful person and deserved to suffer in some manner
of horrific way.

Unless you are the target of such harassment you mercifully
know nothing of how it really feels. I felt paranoid constantly
and the messages just compounded this. I knew these people
knew me but I did not know them. Every person I met on the
street could have been the ones threatening to hurt or kill me.
Strangers felt dangerous. I felt ceaselessly unsafe, yet I had to
keep working on those streets. I felt nervous walking to my car
after work, my hand constantly on a personal alarm the police
had given me. My home was no longer my sanctuary. When
dangerous, deranged, and angry people threaten to hurt you,
you believe them. I was constantly on edge. My city is a small
one. Was the guy looking at me in the supermarket queue the
one who said I should be killed like Lyra was? Was the man

standing behind me in the coffee shop the one who thought I was "lying scum"? Was the man staring at me outside my child's school the one who said he would drag me out of my car? I didn't know, I trusted no one. I feared everyone.

And all the while I was struggling to process intense trauma. At times in those first few weeks I genuinely felt like I was drowning. The whole experience impacted greatly on my mental health. I was grasping at people around me, hoping they could help pull me up. I couldn't breathe at times but still I carried on. I worked day and night to the point of exhaustion. I couldn't stop, because if I stopped I would have to think and I didn't like the horrors that were conjured up in the silence of the night.

Some people, when faced with trauma turn to alcohol, some to drugs. Some take unnecessary risks. I threw myself into work. I needed to always be busy – day and night, all weekend – because when I was busy, I didn't have time to think. When things were quiet, my mind wandered back to that dark Creggan street and the screaming, the sirens, the smoke and the men who meant me and my family harm.

I tried to carry on with my work. I wasn't sleeping at all. I dreaded the night. When I did fall asleep through sheer exhaustion I was having terrible nightmares and night terrors. I often woke up screaming, shouting or gasping for breath. And I carried on my work regardless, out on the street every day. No one knew of my struggle, apart from those closest to me.

I had been to the police on both sides of the border several times over threats and had to pay to have extra security put in place at my house. I was advised to take extra security measures when out. My children were told of the dangers and where they could and couldn't go for their own safety. I removed all pictures of my kids from social media. The police regularly patrolled the area around my house. I gave my teenagers personal alarms.

Some of my friends walked away, perhaps because they didn't understand, perhaps because they didn't know what to say or perhaps they didn't really care that much. I wasn't much fun to be around. I didn't socialise in my own town because of fear of attack and not feeling safe. I barely went out of the house except for work. I had become somewhat of a misery corre-spondent. I'd been on a journey most people couldn't possibly comprehend, nor would I want them to.

I paid a trauma counsellor to listen to me. Some weeks I paid him just to sit in his office and I'd cry for a full hour. The numbness had worn off and I just felt broken.

Only Emmet, who had seen what I saw, understood completely. We held each other up over endless cups of tea. And in the dark of the night, when I felt the world was so full of hate and horrible people who meant me harm, the memory of him running towards danger and putting his coat under a total stranger's head to give her comfort in her final moments was a little light in the darkness.

There was an election two weeks after the shooting. I wasn't equipped for how the world just kept turning. Something horrific had happened and I was carrying around the vivid images of that brutality with me as well as intense paranoia that a lot of people wanted to attack me. I couldn't quite compute that people around me just kept on living life as normal even though this monumental, horrible thing had happened, the harrowing memories seared into my brain.

At the election count people I hadn't seen since the killing didn't want to bring the subject up. Some avoided me completely. Others just blurted out random details they had heard, talking to me about what happened like it was a movie they had seen, asking me if this gruesome detail was true or that.

I was getting terrible, crushing flashbacks. I was doing hourly bulletins for the radio and in between I'd find a quiet corridor to go to and just try to take deep breaths and calm down. I cried in the toilets, washed my face and went back out and did my job. I spoke to politicians, tried to function as a normal human being whose body wasn't wracked by anxiety and panic attacks.

A few weeks later word came through that there was more rioting in Creggan at a bomb scare. I felt dread rise in my stomach and tried to ignore it. I had lived for the news for over 20 years. I loved it and it defined me. It was who I was. I feared nothing. I just got the job done. I jumped in the car and went to the scene, not too far from where Lyra was killed. I gathered my equipment and pondered whether I should wear my flak jacket. I could hear the familiar angry shouting in the distance and the sound of breaking glass.

The simple sound of a siren roaring past rendered me frozen to the spot. With a violent wrench it pulled me right back to that dark Creggan street as Lyra's body was ferried away at speed. I could instantly smell the smoke from the burning vehicles even though there was no fire now. My heart began racing and I started to hyperventilate. I gripped the steering wheel as panic rose over me like a wave. I couldn't breathe. I sobbed and sobbed, hiding my face from people walking past the car. People had been messaging me for weeks telling me to "stay strong" and "keep doing a great job" and here I was an emotional wreck who couldn't even get out of her car at a riot. The echoes of the conspiracy theorists rang in my ears. What kind of reporter is she?

I tried to take deep breaths, wiped my face and got out into the rain, business as usual. A radio station I worked with called and put me on live. It was pouring down, there was a mixture of adrenaline and anxiety, the remnants of the panic attack, coursing through my veins. I was breathing like I had just run a marathon. I genuinely felt like I could be physically sick right there in the street. I stood against a gable wall and we began our broadcast. Two minutes in and a controlled explosion going off deafened me and shook the very foundations of the house I was taking shelter at.

"Jesus!" I declared, live on air. I felt shakeable and vulnerable in the field for the first time in my life.

Over the course of my career I had covered some tough stories – inquests, murders, trials, child deaths, pensioners being brutalised in their homes, fires, shootings, bombings, court cases, deaths, awful, heart-breaking tragedies. The emotional barrier that journalists often develop over the years to protect themselves from those gruelling, brutal stories for me had been tumbled completely. There was now no distinction between real life and work. There was no switching off the emotions going out the door and switching them back on when coming home. Every family occasion was stained by negative thought processes.

At my daughter's First Communion weeks later I imagined my little girl in her beautiful dress having to navigate the day without me, because her Mummy had been shot dead. It scared me so much. I might not have been here had I moved a slightly different way that night in Creggan or been targeted by those threatening harm since.

My battered, bruised and dark imagination conjured up images of me lying in our hallway in a pool of blood – shot dead by someone with burning hate in their heart – like so many people had before me in the Troubles. The ghosts of every such story I covered, those people murdered in cold blood at their front doors, came to haunt me all at once.

Stories affected me in ways they had never done. I deeply felt the pain of every mother who has lost a child, of every wife who has lost their husband. For the first time in my career everyone's pain was mine and I carried it home with me, dragging it with me like a decaying dead horse everywhere I went.

I've covered hundreds and hundreds of funerals in my time. I usually sit at the back of the church discreetly and respectfully and relay proceedings paying tribute to a person I never met. It never bothered me. I found myself at one and looked around at the families grieving, at people crying, at others paying emotional tributes, the sad music, the coffin, a young life ended prematurely. The finality of it all. I found myself sobbing, again.

"Did you know him very well?" asked the older lady sitting beside me at the very back of the church when she saw my distress. She offered me a tissue and patted me on the knee. To be honest I wasn't even sure of the deceased's full name, but because I was blubbering like a fool I said "yes, it's just so very sad".

For a year I couldn't sleep properly and I couldn't look at poor Lyra's face in the paper. I would switch over the news when a story about the incident came on. Her death was a global news story and her smiling face would pop up on social media or in a television programme without warning if there was a development in the case. Every single time the images of that night came back to haunt me. I requested that someone else cover developments besides me. I just couldn't face it.

The picture of Lyra as a little girl at her granny's knee, a face of pure innocence staring up from the front page of a newspaper one day in a coffee shop, just broke me. The image of that beautiful little girl, the same age as my own precious daughter, unaware of the horrors that were ahead, haunted my dreams and my nightmares for months.

There wasn't a week that passed where someone wouldn't call and ask me for a quote for a story or to take part in a documentary. I felt it wasn't my place, I just happened to be there as her life tragically ended. I didn't know the girl at all. I said no every time. I didn't want to even think about it, never mind talk about it. I would dread every time something came up in the murder case because the phone calls would start, reporters asking me if I wanted to comment. It brought everything back every time and I felt like I couldn't move on past it.

No, I didn't want to comment. No, I won't ever comment. Thanks anyway, but please don't call again on this. But they did call, every single time.

I look back at photographs of myself before 18 April 2019 and I see a completely different person, maybe someone who thought life could be hard at times, but had no idea really. My husband Brendan, a tough, no nonsense north Belfast man was there in the middle of the night when I woke with nightmares and couldn't breathe. He understood, having seen horrors himself. He was strong and urged me to focus solely on the important things in life – our kids, our future, and that nothing else mattered. He swore he wouldn't let anyone hurt me and I believed him. In his own unique way he picked me up off the floor and stuck my broken pieces together. He made me strong and able for the fight once more.

The worldwide pandemic slowed all our lives down and at one stage brought it to a complete halt. As lockdown was brought in I got sick with suspected Covid and spent two weeks in bed, unable to stand up for more than a few moments. I was forced to rest and in turn think and process what had happened in the last year. I made myself assess what my future should look like.

It was not easy. I loved the news, I had lived the news for 20 years. Being a journalist was what I had wanted to do since I was a little girl. I had worked day and night to build up my career and establish my reputation as a journalist. I had sacrificed so much. Recent death threats were not the first I had received. I had a drawer full of them – as well as Mass cards and bullets, even old school threatening messages with the letters cut out of newspapers – from two decades in the job in Northern Ireland and the various reprobates you meet along the way. I could have wallpapered my living room with those PSNI booklets they give you on how to keep yourself safe while under threat. It never stopped me doing my job. Or perhaps maybe I never stopped my job for long enough to think too much about it.

Something happened on that dark night in the Creggan Estate. It left a terrible, indelible mark on me. After what I saw and I experienced in the aftermath – which had a deep and terrible impact on my family – I could never have found peace on those streets, on any streets. My life had changed forever. I would never be able to erase the memory of what I saw, so I wanted to get as far away from it as possible. Chasing the news, dealing with horrific stories and hate and the heartbreak of others just tortured my already bruised soul. I needed to burn that life – the one I had worked so hard to build, sacrificed so much for – to the ground and start again. Time to reflect taught me that.

I applied for and got a Journalism Lecturer's job at Ulster University. Teaching journalism and lighting a spark in the next generation was always something I had wanted to do and I found a new life away from those streets. After witnessing such brutal violence, I found my peace.

My young journalists give me such an unshakeable hope for the future, hope that had been all but annihilated on that street, by faceless hate-filled men on a night I will never, ever forget.

What was born from a time of navigating trauma is a desire to help others in this industry, to open up a conversation about nurturing good mental health in the newsroom, to form a community and put resources in place to help others. I want to build resilience in our journalists and give young reporters armour for the field. Journalism is one of the most rewarding, exhilarating and, in my opinion, best jobs on the planet and I want young journalists to love it as much and feel it as deeply and passionately as those who have walked the path before them.

Through my work I have met many people traumatised by incidents in their life. In many ways a horrific experience, my own painful journey, has given me ways to connect with other human beings on a different level and put an authentic voice to their suffering.

Experiencing trauma can send you down one or two paths – you can suffer with post-traumatic stress disorder, or indeed experience post traumatic growth. What happened that night changed me forever. It may have broken me temporarily but ultimately it forever altered my perspective and made me more determined to ferociously chase my dreams.

Life is short and precious. I was spared. None of us can waste our time here.

The Decisive Moment

David McIlveen

DAVID MCILVEEN is a Picture Correspondent based in Belfast who has worked across the world for BBC News. In 2021, he was named Camera Operator of the Year by the Royal Television Society, and described as "simply one of the outstanding camera journalists of his generation". When the first wave of the Covid pandemic hit the UK, he reported from the Royal London Hospital as medical teams fought desperately to save lives on the Covid frontline.

*"What do you do when people are just dying
and dying and dying?"*

The mortuary technician sobbed in front of us – we had watched them break at close quarters, and it was awful. In that moment I found myself experiencing a sensation that I had almost forgotten. When I was much younger, at my Grandad's funeral, I had felt the beginning of tears well up, but through a combination of pride and embarrassment, I was determined not to allow myself to cry and suppressed the urge by clenching my jaw tightly shut. I was doing the same thing here, years later – a seasoned senior BBC camera journalist who had experienced war, natural disasters and all types of human strife – having a powerful flashback to a church pew in Killinchy in County

Down, while in the bowels of The Royal London Hospital in east London.

I told myself my reaction was because I thought that any tears might make operating the camera more difficult, but inside I knew that I was afraid of my colleagues seeing, that they might make a judgement about me. So I focussed all the more intensely on the task in hand, as the mortuary worker spun away covering her face, looking for privacy and comfort from her young colleague, I followed her with my lens, the polished glass blank and pitiless.

It's one of those things that people always say about good news footage.

"You can see the exact moment when..."

"You can see the exact moment when the minister realises, he's screwed."

"You can see the exact moment when they realise, it's over."

"You can see the exact moment when she knows she's won."

The decisive moment Cartier-Bresson would call it if it were stills photography. But unfortunately, this wasn't stills photography, it wasn't 1/1000 of a second, this was a person falling apart before our helpless sight. Falling apart because they had just realised the enormity of what had engulfed them.

Peter Cooper was the BBC Network Camera Journalist in Ireland before I did that job. He taught me literally everything I know about the role and for years we worked closely in the bureau, the BBC national news office in Belfast. Like so many people with their heroes, in my mind Cooper is an untouchable legend. Unflappable in a crisis and always where he needed to be when he needed to be there – no matter the risk. He is from a generation of Belfast 'Troubles cameramen' who talk little about how they felt or what kept them up at night, although it is fair to say Peter is more thoughtful and reasoned about most things than just about anyone you could hope to meet. The walls of the old Ireland Bureau office used to be lined with tapes which contained, what we in the TV industry mystifyingly call, 'rushes'. Rushes are the unedited raw footage that come out of a camera after filming, and Peter had an encyclopaedic knowledge of this particular collection in Belfast, mainly because he had filmed most of it himself.

That day we were in the small office with its outdated banks of tape machines and dusty old TV monitors to edit a news story telling the broad sweep of the Troubles in Northern Ireland for a UK audience, a 'new readers start here' package we called them, although we seemed to do them once every couple of months. The weight of unbroadcast and unbroadcastable murder and mayhem on the thin shelves in that little office had never really crossed my mind, although, as we spooled through tape after tape of body parts being scraped off the street by firemen, burned torsos and dead children, I idly began to consider the support that would be put in place for someone working in those conditions today. As part of my musing, I asked Peter what event stuck with him most from everything he had witnessed. At the time I found his answer surprising, but now, having many more years under my own belt, and in the context of the pandemic, I understand it completely.

It was almost noon on a beautiful early summer's day in Lurgan in County Armagh in June 1997, only five weeks before a cease-fire that would spell the beginning of the end of the Troubles. In a narrow lane in the centre of the small town two members of the north Armagh brigade of the Provisional IRA calmly ran up behind two, shirt-sleeved community policemen on foot patrol and shot them in the back of the head at point-blank range.

The officers, aged 30 and 34, were friends as well as colleagues. Both were married, one with three daughters and one with two sons, all aged ten and under.

Even by the horrific standards of the Troubles these killings stood out. They stood out for being so late in the game. They stood out for being so pointless. Peter was sent to cover the funeral of one of the officers. He described filming the murdered policeman's son, who was seven years old, walking quite normally into the church in Lisburn, wanting to chat to his mother, the young lad even glanced over and smiled shyly at the journalists assembled across the road from the church gates.

Peter's camera was running again when the congregation filed back out into the bright sunlight, and through his lens he could see that everything in that boy's life had changed utterly. He was inconsolable with grief, clinging to his mother with tears streaming down his face, gulping for air. I have seen the footage many times and every time I have a strong emotional reaction. It's a level of anguish brought upon a young child so entirely unnecessarily, entirely as political leverage that I find difficult to grapple with. So, it was that. The grief of a seven-year-old boy, that my old friend said stuck with him most from a lifetime of covering the conflict here.

But as Peter described the day to me, frame by frame, as often happens when camera operators discuss their work together, I grasped that it was more than the raw grief that had the impact. It was the change in the child that he found really upsetting. Peter recognised that somewhere between wandering in at the start of the service and being carried out in fierce tears at the end, that little boy realised that his Daddy wasn't coming back. You can see the exact moment when his tiny world collapsed. The enormity of events had overtaken him, the awful decisive moment.

It's hard to hold a camera in someone's face when they break down in tears. It's hard not to follow your natural human reaction and turn away, embarrassed with the situation. It's hard not to put the camera down and console them. That would be the decent thing to do, right? The only moral and human thing to do? Possibly true. Each bitter, difficult, experience I have of this proves that it can only be judged on a case-by-case basis. There is no catch-all rule and often, when the dust settles, everyone involved decides it is better to include the emotional images to highlight the importance of the story and to show the intensity of feeling at the time – but difficult as it is to film someone in tears, it is much, much more difficult to film them powerlessly as they die.

The sensory overload of working in a Covid ICU ward operating at full tilt is hard to describe. It is sweltering under the vast amounts of PPE, machines bleep, people shout, ventilators pump, it's so busy there is nowhere to stand. Your visor steams up, your goggles and mask dig into your face and for the first two visits we made to The Royal London Hospital there was no vaccine. At this point everything about Covid was still relatively unknown, so there was a real, deep-seated fear of contracting the disease, or carrying it out with us into the community at the end of shift.

Our small team was quite overwhelmed on the first day of our initial visit. It was early in the initial wave of the pandemic and the Royal London Hospital in east London had become the Covid centre for that part of the city. Unfinished floors and storage spaces in the fairly new hospital were desperately being converted into Covid wards while staff rushed to-and-fro pushing lifesaving equipment and trolleys stacked with boxes of supplies. We heard time and again that the hospital was operating at the limit, but we didn't need to be told – we could see it, we could feel it.

The hospital trust had, very unusually, agreed to allow us to embed ourselves with the staff in the Covid ward for almost two weeks. We found a hotel right next door that had been opened to provide accommodation for the NHS staff pouring in from around the UK as this massive hospital put itself on a war footing. It was called a hotel; it was a room in a hotel. All services were closed, and people avoided each other in the corridors. And with good reason. This place contained no-one but NHS staff, an outbreak here would have had critical knock-on effects to the staffing of the hospital. And so, this odd joyless ghost of a hotel became our home for six weeks during the first wave. Totally isolated in the evenings with the ever-present concern of contracting the strange new disease and having no option but to lock ourselves in our room and wait. Wait to see if our symptoms got better or got worse. Having seen the wards up close I'll easily admit to spending sleepless hours wondering if I was feeling hotter than usual, or if my throat was getting a little sore, while simultaneously trying not to think about the intubation procedures, where a tube from the ventilator is pushed down a patient's throat, that we were witnessing day and daily.

In the close-up rushes from our interview camera it is easy to see the physical marks being left on the young staff by the first wave of the pandemic. Masks had gouged deep red sores into their cheeks, exhausted eyes glanced nervously around the room as we made the final adjustments to our recording equipment.

But this perceptible strain was only the surface. Broken is how one described herself to us. Physically scarred, mentally broken, worked to the point of exhaustion only to trudge home alone, through a locked-down London for a restless night much like my own, yet they weren't on a short embed, they were here until the bitter end. Despite all this, during our first period in the hospital it seemed there was a resolve to the staff, a quiet determination to see this thing through. We watched them tenderly holding the hands of dying patients time after time during their working day, then they would hug each other through their protective equipment, exchange a tearful glance and dive straight back in.

We had radio mics on the doctors, so I could hear them from across the room as they whispered to each other that a patient we had been filming with earlier "wasn't going to last the night", and, with permission from his family, we recorded as the frantic efforts around his bed slowly ceased, the insistent alarms were silenced one by one, and he quietly died.

What is expected of a camera journalist in these circumstances? There is an important public health message to convey certainly, one that even the relatives wanted to get across – yet to be present at a moment like this is such a huge thing.

The line between recording images which may ultimately influence public behaviour for the better and overstepping into morbid voyeurism is a fine one. It weighed heavily then and still does.

I spent a lot of time in those long sleepless nights at the hotel thinking about the relatives of the patients we had filmed, the kind looking gentleman we had watched slip away, the middle-aged lady heavily sedated and on a ventilator. What were those families doing right now? Were they scared, angry, hopeful? Did they realise how compassionate the staff were around their loved ones? How would I be feeling if it was someone close to me who was slowly deteriorating?

It is such an enormous responsibility to be allowed access to the most intimate and desperate time in someone's life that, even after only two weeks, I remember thinking that the staff must be wired differently from me, they must be tougher, stronger, because they just kept going – day after day – the dying and dying and dying was becoming as regular as the rhythmic pumping of one of "the London's" priceless ventilators.

"I've been speaking to them, things are getting properly out of hand." Sam is one of the best producers in the BBC, and when he says a story is big, you know it's big. He had been in regular contact with the hospital since our first visit and, after a busy autumn for our small team covering the US elections, the alarm bells were beginning to sound once more. I had just finished a locked-down family Christmas with our young kids, and here we were again, travelling back to the Royal London to revisit the staff and see how the hospital had come to terms with the new normal. I expected something similar, a stoic staff struggling on with a hug and a smile, and the reports of the demise of the NHS to be somewhat jumping the gun. What we found shocked me on a personal level, things were so on the edge in that hospital that I began to worry about the system more generally, and how a total collapse could begin to affect my own family.

There was a heavy frost on the ground as we stamped our feet and watched as the huge crane swung the refrigeration container into the car park of a little mosque in east London. We visited this place multiple times over the next few days as those featureless white boxes slowly filled with the bodies of Covid victims from that part of the city, many of them direct from the Royal London. This emergency morgue was a pretty grim visual representation that something unusual was happening for sure, however we couldn't stay long on that first day as we also had an appointment to film at one of London's biggest burial grounds. As we hoisted our small camera high on a tall pole for an overhead shot, the scale of what was unfolding truly hit us. Row after row of freshly dug graves stretched off to the boundaries of the graveyard, while beside us overworked gravediggers puffed heavily in the cold morning air and grumbled about their huge increase in workload.

All the signs were there, but it was in the long white corridors of the Royal London, still stacked with boxes and equipment, that the tsunami reached its peak, staff struggling to keep their faces above the churning surface, the high tide reflected on the ward ceiling.

We watched as the nightshift doctors realised there were no beds available anywhere in the hospital and followed them on their exhausting rounds through darkened wards. It was on these rounds, at around 2am in a nondescript corridor that we encountered a husband who, moments earlier, had lost his wife to Covid. While I filmed and my colleague Clive comforted the man, he read aloud a letter to his dead wife from his daughters and, choking back tears, showed us his favourite photograph of her. Recording these frail deeds felt to me like a continuation of the tender final scenes we had filmed inside the Covid wards almost a year earlier, and it was no less difficult to watch. This devastated man wanted us to film him, he wanted the world to see the results of this disease, however, as I had been finding time and time again, to put a lens close to the face of someone as they grapple with a grief so fresh, so raw, that they look completely lost, requires a blend of absolute empathy and a hard learned detachment, if only as a personal shield. I was glad to have my eye buried in the viewfinder behind the camera, I find it impossible to know what to say at a time like this.

The next day, at the end of a short call, the senior consultant abruptly put the phone down, pushed her chair back from the desk in the busy Intensive Care Unit and, with tears in her eyes, ran. Ran from our lens, ran from the sympathetic glances of her colleagues. It was a call to the young wife of a man who was on a ventilator on her ward but had gone into steep decline.

"I'm sorry to say, he might not make it," a line she had delivered on countless occasions over the course of the pandemic, but this one time it was too much. Even with her vast amount of experience, it was too much. The enormity of events had overtaken her. It was a scene we witnessed playing out again and again on that second visit. Nurses crying in staff rooms, having to give each other pep talks just to get through a shift.

Exhausted eyes looking straight through the spectacular London skyline just outside the ICU windows. In a quiet moment I found myself staring at that same view, pondering what a strange position it was for us as television journalists to be in – we were exhausted too and with our own stresses and mental strains. As an experienced international news team, we were well used to these feelings, but this was a scenario that we were not familiar with. Not devastation in a foreign field but on our own doorstep, with people dying and suffering all around us. Of course, the unique circumstance meant we couldn't hesitate, couldn't be tired, couldn't turn down access when it was offered at some effort by the staff – so we were running on empty, worried about our families at home, worried about our own health, worried about the staff, while also having to make news reports that were editorially robust and creatively did justice to the people who shared their stories. It was under this strain that we found ourselves in the morgue deep in the basement of the high-rise hospital. Rows and rows of bodies, all with a story, most with a family at home. And suddenly she was crying, crying because this was the first time someone had stopped her and asked if she was OK. Crying because it was all too much. The awful decisive moment.

You can't override your own humanity

Claire Allan

CLAIRE ALLAN was a reporter on the *Derry Journal* for 17 years. She is now a successful crime author.

"I will never forget the animalistic howl of grief."

August 1999 and it was my first day as a staff reporter for the *Derry Journal*.

The month before I had graduated with a Masters Degree in Newspaper Journalism. I had freelanced for a year while I wrote my Masters Dissertation and now I was ready to become a proper journalist.

For me, that meant a job at the *Derry Journal*, a very well-respected local title. I'd done my work placement there while studying and I was ridiculously proud to be joining the staff.

I was taken under the wing of then Deputy Editor Siobhan McEleney, who was an incredible mentor. She believed in me more than I believed in myself. So on that first day she tasked me to the sleepy seaside town of Buncrana in County Donegal. My assignment was to speak to the mother of Sean McLaughlin, who was 12 years old when he died in the bomb attack in Omagh carried out by the Real IRA on 15 August 1998, which killed 29 men, women and children, including a woman with unborn twins.

The first anniversary of the atrocity was that coming weekend and, as you can imagine, emotions were raw.

I remember sitting in the living room of the McLaughlins' home and asking questions which felt at best silly and at worst cruel.

I was asking a mother to relive her trauma. Asking her how she felt when she got the news her son was caught up in the bomb. Asking her to go over the details of that day again. I promised her, and myself, I would make the story about the wee boy Sean had been before he became ever associated with that dark day in our history.

She recalled the day in detail and I scribbled in my brand new notepad. When she told me about his watch and how, due to the catastrophic nature of his injuries, this was how his father had been able to identify his remains, I remember feeling my world tilt a little on its axis.

When we were finished the interview, Sean's mum asked me had I worked for the *Derry Journal* for long. I replied, telling her it was my first day, and I saw sympathy in her eyes. "Oh God, you poor thing. I'm so sorry," she said – this woman who was approaching the first anniversary of her child's brutal murder. I think her compassion towards me broke me even more.

Shortly after, I was picked up from the house by our staff photographer who drove me back to the office. I cried in her car. It would be the first of many times that my job would reduce me to tears. The mental image of a father only recognising his son because of his watch was the first of many horrific images to take up residence in my head.

As I sit down to write this, I realise I don't have a big dramatic story to tell. I didn't find myself caught up in the middle of a riot, or in the immediate aftermath of an explosion. But I spent 17 years working as a journalist. I did my share of death knocks. I attended a staggering number of funerals – there was one ten-day period in which I attended three funerals of people who had died in tragic circumstances. I frequently covered courts, and inquests. I, like my colleagues, never knew who was going to be on the end of the phone when I picked it up.

For me, there was no one big moment but there were tens of little moments that chipped away at my mental health until finally, I knew the job was no longer for me.

It's the details that get to you, you know, much more than the big picture. Tiny moments that stick in your brain and refuse to leave. There are moments now which I can recall with no hesitation – and in journalism we don't have the time to process these. We hit our deadlines and we move on. In local journalism the strangeness of the set up means you can be interviewing a panto actor one moment and standing by the side of the road looking at a pool of blood from an attempted murder the next. And then we go home, and try to act normal, as if everyone hears what we hear every day.

I was in the office one morning. It was an early shift, probably a publication day. I do remember it was grey and gloomy, but then it was always kind of grey and gloomy in the old Buncrana Road offices of the *Derry Journal*.

My phone rang and I answered it, chirruping my introduction: "Hello, Newsroom."

A muffled voice came back to me. A woman with a Derry accent slightly modified with an American twang spoke.

"I want to tell you a story," she said, "about an abuser."

Her words were slurred and it was soon evident that she had been drinking.

"I've not told anyone this, but I want to tell you. I want the *Derry Journal* to write about it and tell people what he did."

I asked the appropriate questions – had she reported the abuse to the police, had her abuser been prosecuted.

"No," she said. "I didn't tell anyone, but I have to tell someone now because I'm going to kill myself. I can't live with this anymore."

By this stage, the lady was sobbing openly and I knew my job had just switched from being a journalist to being the person this lady had reached out to when she was in crisis. I felt a deep, heavy responsibility to say the right thing and to help her out but I also felt woefully inadequate.

I kept her talking. She told me she was in America, where she had been living for decades. None of her family there knew about her abuse. It was this heavy secret she carried around with her. But now, in the wee hours of the morning, in her home in America, while drunk it had become too much for her. My heart ached for her. I wasn't trained in how to help her but I knew she was so distressed that I had to try and talk her down in some way.

I sat at my desk shaking each time her distress ramped up a notch, and deflating with relief when she started to calm down. I handled it the best way I could. I told her of an organisation in Derry who provided support for adult survivors of childhood abuse and passed their details on. By the time, almost an hour later, that we ended the call she had promised she would call them. I did follow this up later and found she had indeed reached out for support.

I was mentally and emotionally exhausted. One colleague said: "That's not our job, you know," as if my talking to her was wrong but I couldn't have, in good conscience, ended the call with her without trying to help her in some way.

I realised that day that for all my years of trying to maintain objectivity as a journalist, you can't override your own humanity.

It had only just gone 9am. The day was still just starting. There was no time to process, or even talk about the weight of responsibility I'd felt. And therein lies one of the biggest problems in journalism – there is still little understanding of the mental health impact our jobs can have. It's a hardnosed, old school culture still. We report. We move on. We don't get involved. I remember being told by a colleague, while I was still studying journalism: "You are not social services. Don't get involved."

I felt it a character flaw in me that I simply could not observe. I couldn't not reach out and cry with someone, or hug them, or offer advice. I started quite quickly to realise that it meant I probably wasn't cut out for all the job entailed. I could not leave stories in the office. They came home with me.

When my son was little, I was tasked to cover an inquest in Limavady. The subject of the inquest was the death of a 22-month-old baby boy from Derry. He had died in June 2006, having become entangled in the blind cord in his bedroom. He was the same age as my son, save for a couple of months.

The court heard how the boy's parents had given him his bottle and put him to bed. It was the same routine I was carrying out with my child every night – the same routine most parents follow.

When his mother went to check on him later she found him at the window, the cord from the vertical blinds around his neck and his head lolling forward.

He could not be resuscitated. I sat in the press bench of that courtroom and listened to his mum sob as she recalled that night and my stomach was turning with grief for her. There were two other reporters in the press bench, both very seasoned male journalists with a lot more experience than I had. They remained stoic while I cried.

The press bench in that particular courtroom faced the bulk of the room, the public gallery, the benches for counsel. There was nowhere to hide my tears, and yet I was also aware this wasn't my story. This wasn't my pain. I was acutely embarrassed at my reaction.

When a policeman gave evidence on attending the hospital to oversee the official identification of the young boy's body, he told the court that when he entered the room, the child's mother was cradling her deceased son in her arms and rocking back and forward crying.

That one image, matched by the grief on her face as she sat in front of me, has probably haunted me more than any other in my career. It was the first time I felt as if I have intruded on someone else's grief. It was the first time I felt like the stereotype of a scumbag reporter – especially when I was asked to doorstep the boy's mother to ask if she wanted to say anything more to the press. The way she looked at me, and shook her head before turning away, tore at me.

I went home that evening and immediately cut all the blinds in my house, and I hugged my son more fiercely than before and I wished I could erase the image of a mother's raw grief.

In 2013, an 11-year-old boy with a heart condition had collapsed and died while playing at a building site. He had died at the scene.

I covered that story for the *Derry Journal*, from checking out the scene of his death, to speaking to the housing association who owned the site, to speaking to his grieving uncle and then to attending his funeral.

Funerals come with the territory. My approach was always to maintain a respectful distance from the mourners. Find a seat, or spot to stand that is discreet and close to an exit and maintain discretion throughout. The boy's death had sent shockwaves through the city. He was from a respected family. He was a popular little boy. His funeral was always going to test the reserves of even the hardest hack.

I didn't relish going to cover it, but when you take on a story you follow it through to its conclusion. I don't remember what hymns were sung that day, or what readings were read. I don't remember the prayers of the faithful or the homily.

But until the day I die, I will never forget the animalistic howl of grief that his mum let out as her baby was being carried out of the chapel at the end of the Requiem Mass. I had never heard anything like it in my life, and I hope never to hear it again.

As I left the church to walk to my car, I felt my knees buckle under me and again I found myself fighting back sobs, which I let out in my car. Again, this boy was a similar age to my own son. I couldn't escape the comparisons. I am a mother and there's a commonality in experience of motherhood. I felt only a tiny percentage of the horror that his mother was experiencing, but it was too much. I questioned then why I was reporting on this funeral. Why I was making content from this nightmare.

It had a profound and lasting impact on me.

I always felt privileged to be able to tell someone's story, but by that stage I had started to dread what may come next. I didn't know how many more tragedies I could bear witness to, but there is always another tragedy around the corner.

I have a list of names in my head. A list of people who have taken up residence there. Some of them have endured unthinkable loss. Some of them have lost their own battles. I have a gallery of images, a collection of sounds. I have seen people who have been broken and not all of them have been able to put themselves back together again.

I have to remind myself all the time that, as I was told previously, it was never my job to be social services. It was my job to tell a story and nothing more – but I don't know any journalist who can fully detach themselves from what they report or the people they talk to.

The final straw for me came in 2016. I had, at that stage, already decided that I would leave journalism and had applied for voluntary redundancy. No one could have predicted the nature or scale of the tragedy that would hit Derry in March of that year.

On the evening of 20 March, a family was wiped out. Sean McGrotty, his sons Mark, aged 12, and eight-year-old Evan, his mother-in-law Ruth Daniels and her 14-year-old daughter Jodie-Lee, died when their car slid into the water at Buncrana slipway.

The day after the tragedy, a Monday, there was a silence in the newsroom like none I've ever known. It felt to me that even the most experienced, most wizened reporter in that room was struggling to come to terms with the news. It was relatable to all of us. Buncrana is a popular spot for a Sunday drive. Stopping off by the pier, grabbing an ice-cream, these are all things we'd have done and not thought twice about. The nature and the scale of the loss was unthinkable.

And then, as names were released, we made connections. Sean and his wife Louise had frequently spoken to the *Derry Journal* to raise awareness of Evan's Muscular Dystrophy. I had interviewed them both not that long before to raise awareness of the Northern Ireland Children's Hospice.

Mark, their eldest son, had been in my son's class at nursery school. I could recall a picture of them together, dressed up for their end of year show. I think we all felt numb. We knew we had a job to do, but I didn't relish the prospect of doing it.

In fact I remember sitting at my desk, head down, hoping that I wouldn't be tasked to follow the story up. I knew that I wouldn't be able to do it. I didn't feel strong enough to deal with the emotional impact of seeing that grief up close and personal.

All I could think of was the little boy in the school photo with my son – their lives ahead of them and it felt much too cruel that it had been taken away from Mark.

I left journalism, on sick leave with stress, just a couple of weeks later.

I never returned. By June I had signed off on voluntary redundancy and I turned my back on the career I had chased since the age of 16.

Journalism had been my life. I'd done my work experience while at school in *The Sentinel* and the *Derry Journal*. I'd studied for a Masters in Newspaper Journalism, graduating from Ulster University in 1999 and immediately starting in the *Derry Journal*.

I had assumed, and planned, that it would be a job for life. I never expected it to have the emotional impact that it did. That was probably very naïve of me.

There is no time to reflect. The pressure of constant rolling deadlines, and the desire to get the best story as quickly as possible means reporters just have to get on with the job.

Talk of finding certain stories tough is almost frowned on. Certainly, I never felt truly comfortable expressing that a story had upset me. Journalism, for all it has come on, is still very much a male dominated industry and one in which we are expected to remain as neutral in our reactions as we are in our reporting.

The problem then persists when we have no time to process what we have seen and heard until after the paper has gone to print, and we carry that stress and upset home and into our family lives.

By the time I left journalism, I felt broken. That's the only way to describe it. Not only because of the stories I'd covered and the lack of any sort of formal peer support, but also because I felt as if I had singularly failed at my career. I had let it get to me where others seemed to take it all in their stride.

At that stage, I have invested 19 years in a career that I no longer felt suited to.

I remember one of the biggest feelings I had at leaving the job was that I'd not have to cover stories of human tragedy any more. But as the years have passed, I have realised that the details will never leave me. In fact, more and more come back to me. Tiny things. A watch on a young boy's wrist. The phone call from a stranger in a different continent who finally needed to talk. The sound of a mother's anguish. A mental image of a mother cradling her dead baby. The picture of a child dressed for a school show, now dead.

These, and so much more are things I carry around.

They still have the power to reduce me to tears.

A few years before I left journalism, I attended an event to educate and advise journalists on the reporting of suicide. As the session wound to a close one of the advisors said that if any of us present needed to talk about the pressures we faced, his door was open.

"People don't realise the things journalists see," he says. "No one talks about it."

That is my wish for the future of journalism – that there is an open conversation about how tough this job can be. That it is okay to admit that you're struggling. That the powers that be introduce some sort of peer support or debriefing after emotional events. It should never be the case that we send a story to print and move on as if it hasn't touched us in some way.

I've seen too many good journalists burn out before their time because of these pressures. And I've heard the way journalists with mental health issues are talked about. We're not up to the job.

We would be, and more, if we were supported properly in our industry. Journalists, especially good journalists, are not disposable. We're not a dime a dozen. It takes years to make a great journalist, and only one traumatic event to break one.

I don't regret leaving journalism. I have forged a new career, writing fiction. Writing crime novels has given me a way to exorcise some of my demons. It has been cathartic to explore emotions in shades of dark and light. I am, dare I say it, happy in my career now.

But for all those journalists coming up through the ranks. Those who haven't had their wristwatch moment yet, we need to do more.

Staring down the muzzle of a gun

Neil Mackay

Originally from Antrim in Northern Ireland, Neil Mackay was editor of Scotland's *Sunday Herald*, where he is currently writer-at-large. He has written several critically acclaimed books and produced a number of TV and radio documentaries – this essay was originally published in the *Sunday Herald*.

> *"I made foolish jokes out of what was eating me alive
> from the inside out."*

Sometimes all it takes is the smell of nicotine from someone's clothes, and I tumble back through whatever internal time machine operates inside my head to find myself staring into the barrel of a gun – the mouth of the muzzle a black hard empty circle like the heart of a black hole. The fingers on the hand holding the gun stink of stale cigarettes, and there's a black rind of old hashish under the fingernails. I watch those fingers as they curl around the trigger and squeeze – the gun ready to fire straight into my face.

Psychologists call it a flashback. I call it one of my slip-away moments. I might be sitting in a restaurant and someone will walk past me who's been smoking outside. I catch the whiff of nicotine from them, unexpectedly, and I'm back in 1999.

I'm 29 again and I'm sitting in the living room of a loyalist terrorist in Northern Ireland. He chain-smokes cigarettes and joints. I smoke myself but the continual reek of his cigarette is starting to make me feel sick. I've known this man quite some time. I'm a reporter, and covering Ireland and paramilitary violence is one of my specialities. I come from Northern Ireland but I live in Scotland and write for Scottish newspapers. Every time I travel to Northern Ireland to cover some murder or bombing or rioting, I meet up with a selection of paramilitary contacts so I can understand what's going on with republican and loyalist terrorists. This man is one of these contacts.

I arrived at his house a few hours ago and we've been drinking. I've had a few, and he's had too many. He's also started to smoke joints, crumbling hash into Rizla papers on the table that sits between us. He's drunk and a little high and he's also got a gun on the table. The Good Friday Agreement may have been signed last year previously, supposedly bringing peace to the country, but there's still killing. A solicitor called Rosemary Nelson, who represented republicans, had been murdered not long ago, and there's a sense that the North could erupt again. That's why I'm here.

Ostensibly, I've met this contact to talk about what's going on within loyalist terrorist organisations, but I'm also interested in him. I like to write about more than just the bare facts of the news. I want to include some human dimension in my reporting, so I always try and find out what makes these killers I speak to tick. What's a gunman like when he's being a dad; what's a terrorist commander do when he goes shopping with his wife? These questions interest me. I tell myself that I'm trying to understand the men behind the monsters so readers can understand them too.

My contact has a son aged around eight. He loves him with the fierce passion that only a dangerous man can love their child. We've been talking for hours and he's been fidgeting with his pistol all the while – cleaning it, taking it apart and putting it back together again, putting bullets into it, taking bullets out again. There's weapons all over his house. The windows are bullet-proof glass, and it would take a tank to get through the reinforced steel front and back doors.

I feel I've come to know this man well enough over the years to ask questions which might reveal a little more about him as a human being rather than just a gunman and terrorist. So I ask him about his child. Does he worry that the life he lives might influence his son, that his kid might grow up to be like him?

There's times when you can see violence in the eyes of another man. My contact slowly looks at me and those eyes narrow – he holds my gaze, hard like a strangling grip, and there's not a word spoken.

"What did you say?" he asked – but it was no question.

I realised I'd gone too far. I'd insulted him. A cold, slow sensation, like iced water, flowed through my body as I thought of the locked steel doors, the unbreakable windows. He was drunk, he was stoned. There was a gun on the table. I could feel violence on him.

I apologised and said I didn't mean to upset him. It was a silly question.

He never broke his stare. His hand moved and I looked down. He picked up the pistol on the table in front of him.

"You're a fucking cunt," he said.

I was saying something like, listen, I'm sorry, I didn't want to offend you.

"I like to kill cunts like you," he said.

I called him by his name and said, "We've known each other for years, come on."

He raised the gun now and pointed it straight in my face, the barrel was less than an inch from my nose. It was all I could focus on – the black hole of the muzzle where the bullet comes from.

"I'm going to fucking kill you," he said. "And I'm going to enjoy it."

The hand holding the gun was so close to me that I could smell the nicotine from his fingertips, and see thin half moons of dry black hashish under his nails. I watched as his finger curled around the trigger and I saw the metal move. I didn't even have time to beg or say please don't kill me, I've got two daughters. The finger tightened and the trigger went back hard and fast.

There was no bang. Just a click. Then he started to laugh.

"You should have seen your fucking face," he said.

He'd slipped the bullets from the gun and dry fired the empty chamber in my face. He'd put me through a mock execution for a laugh.

"You're a good lad, Neil," he said, still laughing. I laughed too. Was it funny? I couldn't tell. I sat drinking with him for another hour and then left. I put what happened out of my head. Or thought I did.

A few years ago, now in my late 40s, I thought I was having a cardiac arrest. My heart was racing, my chest ached. I was terrified. The doctor checked me over and told me there was nothing organically wrong with me – but my heart rate was going crazy at times.

"Maybe you're having panic attacks," she said. "Anxiety?"

Stupidly, arrogantly, I thought I was made of stronger stuff than that, but obeyed my doctor when she referred me to a psychologist to see if there was something up. Deep down I knew all wasn't right. That psychologist took my mind apart like it was a Lego toy. I can't even remember the path she followed with her questioning but before I knew it she had me talking about my experiences with violence throughout my life.

I found myself talking about being in a bomb blast as a kid – about growing up on a rough and tumble housing estate in Northern Ireland in the middle of the Troubles as a teenager in the 80s and the sense of menace that saturated everything. I told her how I'd been nearly beaten to death aged 14 by a gang of skinheads. They'd kicked and stamped on me and tried to kill me and only stopped when an off-duty police officer who lived in a nearby house came out with his weapon drawn.

I told the psychologists I went a bit off the rails after that. I could have easily drifted into a life of petty crime and violence, but I got myself back on track after a few years. The one thing that saved me was my brains. I was clever at school and as O Levels approached, I put my head down and watched the A grades come in. I wanted more success then, as I knew that would get me out and away from where I lived, from all that violence and ugliness. I got the marks I needed and won myself a scholarship to Queen's University.

Not long into first year, a gang of loyalists attacked me and a group of my Catholic friends (I'm from a religiously mixed family and couldn't care what church you go to) outside a student nightclub. I was kicked senseless and beaten around the head with two by four timbers. When I woke up in hospital, a cop told me I was lucky I wasn't dead.

I told the psychologist that I became a journalist in Northern Ireland but moved to Scotland after I received death threats for my reporting. I wanted to get married and have a family in a country where we all felt safe. But my work as a writer always centred on violence and violent men – it was like I couldn't let go of violence. I needed to explore it. Was I obsessed with it too? Trying to work something out?

I found that I couldn't stop talking to the psychologist. I told her that I felt violence had stalked me my whole life. I told her about the mock execution, I told her about being abducted as a reporter in Northern Ireland and held by gunmen with a bag over my head.

I told her that throughout my life I'd tried to drown out memories of all these things in self-destructive ways. Drink, drugs, sex, work – these are all ways to fill your mind up with experiences right here in the present moment which mean you can't think of the past. There were times when I felt like the luckiest person on the face of the Earth and other times when it felt like some black gelatinous blob had consumed me and eaten me whole.

I felt myself getting tearful as I explained how thankful I was that my behaviour had only damaged myself over the years, and not those I love. But at times, I must have been so hard to live with and love. I told her that the worst thing is that sometimes I've turned these events that happened to me into after dinner stories – I made foolish jokes out of what was eating me alive from the inside out.

The terrible thought that I can't get out of my head, I said, is that other human beings inflicted damage on me, and changed me, and there's nothing I can do about it. It's like they still live inside my head or my soul. I've never wanted to hurt another human being, but I'd happily kill those men with my bare hands.

They come to me when I have these slip-away moments, I told her. I could be lying on the couch listening to music and something would prompt a memory of a gun or a boot or a hood, or screaming or crying, and I'd be back in that moment as if I'd time travelled. And there were always the same repeating thoughts: "You could have died. How did you not die? Imagine if you'd died."

Then I'd physically shiver and judder as I expelled the thoughts and memories from my mind – like a dog shaking water from its fur after swimming in a pond.

The psychologist listened. A kind and considerate woman who I owe a great debt to. She told me simply I had post-traumatic stress disorder.

"It's an incredible amount of violence you've experienced over your life," she said. And she referred me to a specialist in trauma therapy.

I was dazed by the diagnosis. Confused. I didn't like the idea of being medicalised but she'd shown me something was wrong and I knew I needed to deal with it. The appointment arrived for the first session with the trauma specialist. But I didn't go. At the time, I found excuses – this meeting or that meeting – but really, I was too cowardly, maybe too prideful also, to confront what needed to be confronted.

I told no one apart from my closest loved ones about the diagnosis. I changed my lifestyle – slowing down, taking things easier – but did nothing else. It wasn't enough. Nothing should fester.

That was a few years ago now. Then just a few weeks ago, an old friend called Chris Lindsay contacted me. I'd shown him the ropes as a young journalist in Northern Ireland before I left to live in Scotland in the mid 90s. Chris told me that in 2005 he'd been caught up in a bomb attack in Belfast while reporting on rioting. He was badly injured and could have died. It had messed him up. I felt a gush of understanding and empathy for him.

A group of journalists in Northern Ireland were writing about their experiences of PTSD, trauma and physical injury while covering violent conflict. Chris was writing a chapter on what happened to him for the book. He knew I'd written a number of books and wanted me to cast my eye over his work as an author. I was happy to.

I read what he'd written and felt ashamed. If Chris and these other reporters had the bravery to confront what happened to them, why didn't I? I feel sorry for men who can't show their feelings – now I was one of them. Why had I refused to even go and see the trauma specialist? Why had I kept this all buried inside?

I knew the answer. I was scared of seeming weak. I knew so many people who'd suffered so much more than me. How could I complain? My experiences were nothing compared to people who've lost their loved ones, to reporters who've been shot.

But there was nothing weak about Chris honestly explaining in his writing how exposure to violence had damaged him – both mentally and physically. In fact, it was the reverse of weakness. It was brave.

I told Chris about what happened to me. I said I didn't have the courage to do what he'd done. He told me courage was the wrong word. It's not about being brave, it's about being honest and confronting what happened to you. Speaking about it and writing it all down was therapy, he said.

So that's why I've written this. I'm going to go back to my original psychologist and ask them to set up an appointment with the trauma specialist I failed to visit. And then I will see what happens.

The most insane job

Natasha Sayee

NATASHA SAYEE was a broadcast journalist for 17 years, mostly with the BBC, where she was a News Correspondent for BBC Northern Ireland and network outlets – interviewed by Leona O'Neill

> *"It felt like there was a spectre walking behind me, that I couldn't see, but it was always there."*

Michaela McAreavey was strangled to death at the luxury Legends Hotel resort in Mauritius in January 2011. The 27-year-old teacher was on her honeymoon with her husband John when she was murdered in her hotel room after disturbing a burglar. Two former hotel workers were acquitted at her murder trial in 2012. The family continue to seek justice.

I know that had I not covered Michaela's murder case, I probably would still be a journalist. I'm really glad that I'm not anymore. It's a different life for me now. That trial changed my life. It wasn't just the trauma, it just opened me and changed me in so many different ways.

I had always wanted to be a presenter. From when I was five years old, I was doing speech and drama, winning awards in the local arts festivals. As soon as I could work a recorder,

I was doing interviews. I got myself a JVC camera and I made my own videos. I auditioned to join MTV.

I kind of fell into journalism more than anything else. I was studying law at university, because my parents had hoped I'd do it. I'm from a traditional Indian family where you're either a doctor, lawyer or engineer and you have no choice. When I was at law school I realised, probably in the first week, that it wasn't for me. I used to stand outside BBC Broadcasting House with my friends and I would say to them, "I'm going to work in there one day". I didn't know how I was going to get in there, but knew I was on the right path. Cool FM were looking for presenters, I applied there, got the job, and I loved it.

What led me into journalism was one night I was starting the 1am shift on Cool FM, I might have been 18 years old. The news came on – which at that time I never listened to – and I had my track list there waiting to go after the bulletin. The first song I played was The Cars Who's Going To Drive You Home?. I played the track and the then deputy news editor called me straight away and asked me if I was stupid. He asked if I hadn't listened to the news. I hadn't. There had been a car crash and several people had died and the first song I played was that one. I was shaking in the studio, thinking about the tragedy and my ignorance, and from that moment on I never missed a news bulletin.

I finished my law degree and kept up the presenting, went on to do a Broadcasting MA and came back to Northern Ireland where I became a senior broadcast journalist with the BBC. And I thought that was it, I had achieved my dream.

I covered many stories. I covered the Stephen Carroll trial. The Continuity IRA murdered the police officer in 2009. That was a particularly tough one and just after my Dad died. The first story I had to do was cover the killing of a man shot in

Templepatrick. I had to interview his family. I was really young and I felt the impact of those in particular.

But most of the time as a broadcast journalist, my way of coping was to develop a persona, and it felt very much like I was observing things in a movie. That is how I dealt with all trauma, even right down to my Dad's funeral. I remember thinking, I'm watching this in a movie, I could almost see the movie playing out. It's a separation technique and I think it helped me to separate myself from all the trauma associated with journalism. It's like I had this protective glass case or wall around me, nothing could get in.

I think you do desensitise when you are faced with the harrowing things we can see as journalists. But I also think you have to have some humanity in terms of how you deliver when you are broadcasting. I think one of the reasons I left journalism was not the struggle with delivering empathy, but that for me it became a pattern: my inflections, everything became quite robotic in the end. I was doing the same thing over and over again. You're going to people's houses in the midst of their life crisis, and you have this pressure on you to get it done quickly and well, and the best story while trying to be empathetic. It is just the most insane job.

Up until the Michaela McAreavey murder trial I loved my job. I was getting really good stories, really good exposure, getting well known, finding my place in Northern Ireland. I was doing BBC Northern Ireland news shifts and was filling in as Ireland Correspondent when asked. I had a huge range of network contacts. That was my life. I absolutely lived for that job. I lived off adrenaline. I never really switched off. I was always on Twitter, always searching and investigating. I was always on, continuously. And it's only when I left that life behind that I realised that I was a total adrenaline junkie.

I didn't know Michaela McAreavey at all. I didn't cover the murder itself. A colleague did. It felt to me like no more or less brutal than other things at the time, and that is awful. Obviously, everyone was shocked because of who Michaela was and what had happened, but for me at that time – and I think that this just shows how the glass case protects us as journalists – following it up was just a story like others I had done before. Reflecting later I remember how this position shifted and how my empathy for the family developed into real sadness for them.

At the time I saw it as an opportunity for me to continue on the upward trajectory that I was on within the BBC.

But about six months before the trial was called, I remember thinking that no one was really looking at this case. I wanted to know where it was sitting, when it was going to work its way through the system in Mauritius. I started reaching out. I used my middle name, which is an Indian name, and I used my law credentials to contact the prosecution service and the defence lawyers. I started making the contacts, and getting the dates, and forming the stories. The Planning Editor said that as I was following it, I was over the story and asked if I would go to the trial. I had my bag packed in two seconds. Back then, travelling was no problem for me. I was up and down the road on any story they wanted. Travelling didn't bother me. I was young, I wanted to get out there and do the job and I was delighted to get the opportunity.

I went out to Mauritius early to try to get some context and background and familiarise myself with the place and the people. I just thought that I was in a really strong position, days ahead of the trial starting, for the BBC to really own this story locally. That is what it was to me. It was about the BBC delivering for the consumer, for its audience, and getting the information before any of my competitors out there. I was very much a lone wolf: it was me and my cameraman against the world, I didn't care about the rest of the media. We were getting this for us and for the BBC. But what happened over the next ten to 12 weeks made me realise that I had to work in partnership with and collaborate with, care for and look after the people I worked alongside. And it opened up a world of relationships that I didn't have before.

I remember standing outside the trial, getting bitten by mosquitos, thinking it's me against the world, being first at the gate in my red dress and high heels, with my camera. I was even very particular about who I shared information with, opened up to. It was just such a competitive environment. I remember one time freezing on a job on the north coast of Northern Ireland and Tommie Gorman from RTE saying to me and my cameraman to come in to the RTE van to get some heat and I said no, that I was OK, and I stood there freezing instead. But in Mauritius, Tommie became like a Daddy to us all during that horrendous time and he is still a trusted friend and mentor to me to this day. The glass wall that had protected me for so long dropped during that trial. I don't know if it was the endurance of it, or the impact it was having on me and other colleagues. It was absolutely horrific.

One day during the trial, they were showing Michaela's bikini, and I found it absolutely appalling. I looked over and saw a colleague had started to cry and I thought to myself, this is really impacting on people who I thought had tougher glass walls than me. It might have been that we were all away from home. It became very jingoistic. It became the Mauritian media versus us. And I'm not sure if I helped that by starting off on that really competitive foot. What I should have done was to create relationships and partnerships with the Mauritian media instead of trying to blow everyone out of the water to get the story.

And then it became so physically oppressive. There was the heat. The courtroom was absolutely packed. The smell. The way the family were treated. The laughter, the sneering, the looks. What started off as a them and us mentally, became them versus us physically.

I am mixed race, but I was part of a tiny group of white people standing on the fringes, with everyone else in the room not welcoming us, not wanting us to be there, wanting another outcome than there was. There was a really heavy, oppressive undercurrent. You could nearly have taken a knife and cut the air. And this was every single day for 12 weeks. It was outside the court, inside the court.

We were listening to the most horrific details of the murder in the court. I was going back to my hotel room where I felt exposed and vulnerable and nervous. The BBC couldn't have done more for us with regards health and safety, security, looking after us but I still felt vulnerable. I replayed the scenarios in my head. I thought about how Michaela had gone back to her room to get a biscuit and this awful, brutal thing had happened to her. And I could hear people walking around outside my hotel room. Someone might have called to my door with washing or whatever – because we were there for so long – and I'd think every time, what is going to happen here? It felt like there was a spectre walking behind me, that I couldn't see, but it was always there.

There was a real spotlight on us and there really was no hiding. I tried to do things for myself at the weekend by going to get my nails done or whatever and people would say to me that they didn't think I was reporting the trial right and the people were innocent. I just couldn't escape from it, every single day, no matter where I went. I'd be walking down the street and the wives of the accused would chase me waving family photographs and letters from their husband's employers, waving them right in my face, begging and pleading with me to do what I could, that I was the BBC. I was absorbing all this raw emotion and negativity at every turn and there was no let up.

In some ways it might seem like I was lucky, to get out to cover a story in Mauritius. But I stayed in a hotel room for 12 weeks because I was afraid and didn't want to engage in anything. And we saw what could actually happen behind those fortified and secured beautiful hotel walls. I think where I did find beauty, and I couldn't have got through it without them, was in my colleagues. We needed to decompress and look after each other. But still we felt we were under scrutiny so we had to be very careful about how we behaved, about where we went.

I'll never forget those weeks, the smells and the heaviness of the air, and the horror of what we saw in those photos. I came home and I felt great for a while. I felt I had absolutely proved myself and I was the only female who stuck it out the whole time. I thought that was great. After an elation factor of being home for maybe a month, I started to ask myself what the point of any of it was, really. I started to think about the transience of life. I was being offered all these opportunities with the BBC and I just thought 'yeah, but what is the challenge?' There was a Business Correspondent job coming up, people said I should go for it. But I just had no motivation whatsoever. And I was turning up at stories, and it was like I had lost something. I was a shell, but a shell that performed exceptionally well, so no one ever knew. It was getting to the point where I didn't even need to take my notebook out. It was robotic, I had lost all passion for the job I had dreamt about since I was a little girl. I think it was a combination of losing the kick and feeling that your body and brain had been through a food processor and you were totally different by the time the whole thing had ended. And I didn't even realise.

And I just thought, maybe this isn't for me. Maybe I've just done the biggest challenge and there's nothing left to do. I felt empty.

I was exhausted when I came back from Mauritius and I didn't want to travel anywhere, not even down the road. Later that year I was covering the flag protests – thousands of loyalists took to the streets after Belfast City Council restricted the flying of the Union Flag at City Hall – and had got death threats to my home. I was out on a story one night and had been called a "Paki bastard" by a guy wrapped in a Union Flag. This is just six months after I came back from the horrors of Mauritius. My friends were in the pub, just before Christmas celebrating the season, and there I was standing in the street, getting racist abuse. I'd had a death threat sent to my house which came via a Christmas card. And I just thought, that is it. I'm done here.

I looked for another job and I ended up going into PR and to be honest I am a totally different person. Looking back, I would have done things differently. I would have collaborated more with my colleagues, I would have opened up more at the beginning and sought relationships out when I was at a good point rather than when I was drowning with the oppression of it all. In hindsight I wouldn't have stayed in Mauritius for as long as I did. The BBC rang me every week and asked me if I was alright and if I wanted to go home. And I said no.

I haven't dealt with the trauma, and I am only acknowl-
edging it now, with the help of this book. I don't know if I ever
will deal with it. It's a strange one.

For me leaving journalism was like leaving a family, and
it's something that I never acknowledged. I was so focused on
getting away to a bigger or different challenge that I cut and
ran. I would regularly have nightmares, not about Mauritius,
but about my colleagues and reporting. When I think about
that time in my life I think about change, but I also think
about loss a lot. I have learned and grown so much as a person
through this experience, and I was near enough broken during
it. But I came through it, I was resilient, and I have literally
changed my life.

Over a period of six months I canned a career that I had
wanted to do since I was five years old. That is mad. I let things
go very quickly and I wonder how much of that was survival
for me and I didn't realise it. I do miss my journalistic family.
We went through the fires together. We cried together. We saw
stuff together. I think that you have that experience of being a
journalist with your team that you don't have in any other business. And it's the family that I miss. I have no regrets, though. I
don't have to look through that glass wall any more. I don't have
to be that lone wolf.

If I was to pass on any advice to other journalists it would be
not to put up a front. You don't have to be the hardest, fastest,
best all the time. Acknowledge when you need a friend and
when you are struggling. Don't sit in your hotel room with the
door locked, feeling afraid. Go and meet other people. It's not
weakness to ask for help, it actually shows strength in creating
relationships and friendships.

Acknowledge when you are struggling. I want journalists
to know that it's not just bombings and shootings and the like

that can cause trauma. You could be impacted by anything you meet on a day-to-day basis, and you need to talk, you need to share, you need support. Journalists should help each other and look out for each other.

Internal Conflict

Josh Mainka

JOSH MAINKA has covered war and conflict for the past 25 years with Reuters, Sky News and Al Jazeera: he was in Afghanistan after 9/11, Baghdad for the US Invasion of Iraq in 2003, the Arab Spring uprisings in Tunisia, Egypt, Libya, and the battle for Mosul in 2016. He now works for BBC Northern Ireland.

"You learn to cope by numbing your feelings, shutting out the extremes of emotion, knowing that happiness is the yin to the yang of sadness, and I couldn't trust myself with either."

I picked up my phone and tried to focus on the screen through a sea of tears. I was calling for help. I needed help. The phone rang and the receptionist at the Al Ahli Hospital in the Qatari capital Doha answered. Do you have a mental health clinic I asked, my voice weak with desperation. I don't understand she said with a thickly accented Arabic accent, mental health? OK, I replied weakly and hung up, resigned to my fate.

I sat for a few moments, considered my next move and walked to the window of my apartment and opened it, just wide enough to squeeze myself though. I looked down, 22 floors to the road below and an immediate solution to the pain and anguish.

The phone vibrated in my hand; it was the number for the hospital on the screen.

"Hello," a kindly voice on the other end began, I heard my colleague speak to you and I wanted to call you back and say that we can help.

Please can you come to the hospital tomorrow morning?

"Yes," I replied, my hands shaking with the realisation of what I'd been about to do.

I closed the window, sank to my knees, and looked up at the cloudless blue sky, tears running down my cheeks. Fate and a quick-thinking receptionist had just granted me another day. This was March 2017 and four months after returning from covering the Battle for Mosul in northern Iraq with Al Jazeera. Not long after I returned from Mosul my marriage fell apart. That felt like another sudden death, which opened the door to past trauma.

In the days and weeks that followed I descended into the madness of hypomania, keeping relentlessly busy to mask the pain. Neither sleeping nor eating properly before finally surrendering to the darkness of PTSD again, reliving the events of my first brush with its black, icy grip after Baghdad in 2003 when an American tank turned its barrel onto the Palestine Hotel and fired a single round that ripped into the Reuters office, killing my friend, cameraman Taras Protsyuk.

I'd kept a diary in Baghdad, encouraged to document what I was witnessing by my friend, Norwegian correspondent, and author Åsne Seierstad. She had presented me with a notebook and pen on my birthday one week into the war and I had taken to writing each evening as I waited for the next airstrike. The following is my account of the attack on the hotel. Written that night with adrenalin still coursing through my veins, unable to

sleep as American warplanes continued to pound the city. A
day that would come to haunt me.

Baghdad, Tuesday, 8 April 2003

The day had started badly, explosions waking me from an
exhausted sleep at 5am.

I gingerly stepped onto my 14th floor hotel balcony overlooking the Tigris to see three US tanks sitting on the Jumhuriya
Bridge less than a mile away, goading the Iraqi militias on the
east bank of the river into a fight. It was going to be a long day.
I had a quick breakfast from our rations and headed down to
the first floor to fire up our satellite equipment.

This flat section of roof, one floor up and above the confer-
ence centre was a tent city, housing the technical equipment
that allowed Networks to broadcast the television images back
to their audiences. It was also where broadcasters had their live
positions, overlooking Firdos Square where one of the ubiq-
uitous statues of Saddam Hussein dominated the centre of a
traffic roundabout.

Mid-morning and news that the offices of Al Jazeera, close
to the Ministry of Planning, had been hit by either a tank
round or an air strike, killing reporter Tarik Ayoub and seriously injuring his cameraman as they filmed from the roof.

The war was getting very close, and the Palestine Hotel
looked like it was the only safe place left in the city centre. We
had a busy morning filing live reports but during a lull in the
fighting I popped into the adjacent CBS News satellite tent to
offer my condolences to Rifat, an Al Jazeera satellite engineer
who'd been operating the equipment after most of the CBS
crew had left prior to the outbreak of war.

As we spoke, I heard a sound that I instinctively knew spelt
danger, the distinctive sound of an incoming shell.

"Down, Down!", I shouted, verbally pushing Rifat and CBS News correspondent Lara Logan, standing close by, to the ground. Then a bone-shattering explosion, the sound of debris falling all around us, and then for a moment, silence.

I ran back to my satellite tent through the smoke and dust and called the Sky News foreign desk on the satellite phone. "The hotel has just been hit." Then a sound I will never forget, a woman's scream, distorted with shock and fear.

"Oh my God, they've hit Reuters. They've hit Reuters."

One of the tanks on the bridge had turned its barrel towards us, perhaps mistaking the glint of a television camera on a tripod for a rocket launcher and fired one shell, the mile between the tank and its target, our hotel, taking a split second to negotiate.

"Get to the basement, they may fire again," I shouted at anyone that could hear as the dust and the smell of the explosion settled around us, grabbing the first aid kit full of field dressing I had hanging off the tent wall.

I'm running now, breathless, below the damaged balcony and the screams above, past the generators powering our equipment, strewn with pieces of rubble. Down the stairs, people running ahead of me, waiting to enter the elevator.

"Take the stairs," I screamed at them, "stairs, stairs, stairs!"

You really didn't want to be stuck in a lift if another tank round hit the building and the power was cut. Down one flight and I'm running through the hotel lobby and down one more to the sanctuary of the basement. I'm panting and sweating, but I'm safe.

The basement was a throng of Iraqi civilians who had come to seek refuge from the fighting above. Women cradling groups of infants in the folds of their skirts, tears streaming from frightened, innocent eyes. Some of the new arrivals collapsed onto chairs while the rest of us stand, collecting our thoughts with shock written all over our faces.

Why had the Americans targeted this hotel? I take a deep breath and decide to head back upstairs. My friends and colleagues were there, and I had to try and help having had extensive first aid training.

Back up the first flight of stairs again to the lobby, two steps at a time, field dressings gripped tightly in my white knuckled hand to the ground floor, weaving in-between people milling around in the confusion towards the next flight of stairs. As I passed the elevator and stopped as it pinged and the doors opened, painfully slowly as ever. High pitched voices inside were screaming in Arabic, English and Spanish. Bloodied hands, panicked faces carrying an improvised stretcher made of blankets and sheets emerge and start running towards the hotel entrance. Cocooned inside, a lifeless body whose face is immediately familiar through the blood and dirt, it was Taras.

I'm now running beside them, panting, desperate, knowing I had to stop them for a moment to try and arrest the bleeding.

"Bandages, bandages!" I shout.

But no one is stopping, and I feel completely alone.

"Stop. Stop! Bandages, bandages, stop…stop!"

Outside, into the bright sunlight. I'm still running parallel to them, still shouting for them to stop, just for a moment. I could see the lifeless body being placed into the back seat of a car through the crowd and off it went. Bloodied sheets, red like tattered flags billowing in the breeze from an open window. It was impossible to stop them in the chaos.

I'm left feeling helpless, useless, and now I'm almost completely spent as I step back inside the hotel. I hear the elevator bell ping again and the doors open wide, like the serving hatch from Hell. Another dish of blood and guts displayed on a sheet and screaming men running towards the hotel exit. There's no stopping them, panic has no logic. I return to the basement, there's Lara.

"I can't get near them, I can't help them," I pant.

She stands, takes a deep breath and we nod at each before heading back upstairs to the broadcast tents where we have satellite phones and communication with the outside world.

I call Reuters, still breathless, and try to recount what I'd seen and heard so far.

"What are their injuries, where have they been taken?" they ask.

The questions from London were now mixing with those spinning around my head. Why had an American tank fired on the only hotel containing the media in the centre of Baghdad?

Taras sadly dies on his way to the hospital. Jose Couso, a Spanish cameraman, filming on the 14th floor loses a leg in the blast and hours later his struggle for life.

Others from Reuters are seriously injured: Paul, another friend and cameraman; Samia from print; and a stills photographer that I didn't know. I put the phone down as David Chater arrives with Milan and Veljko, the rest of the Sky News team. They'd been on the same floor as Jose, witnessing the chaos first-hand and I was glad to see that they were safe.

"We must go live," he says stoically as we look around at the other empty broadcast positions. We all nod in agreement.

I fire the satellite link and we we're soon live on Sky News with David explaining what had just happened to our viewers. Explosions and small arms fire echoing all around us. Dehydrated with shock, sweat and the tears running down my cheeks I sit quietly in the tent after David had finished his report, my body, mind and heart aching. I step outside and all four of us stand in silence together for a moment lost in our own thoughts.

Veljko's swimming googles, a protection against smoke and dust, are now half filled with his own tears. We light candles for Taras, Jose and Tarik from Al Jazeera that night. Journalists from around the globe standing together in silence on the dry grass in front the hotel.

Still in range of the American tanks, we silently defied them. We felt like the ordinary Iraqis now, candles lighting our faces like the civilians sheltering at home without power or running water. Wondering that when the US 'liberation' finally came, would the price be too high.

The short-term effects of trauma and PTSD are well documented. They include: insomnia; flashbacks of the incident; anger and aggression; feeling numb and empty; being hypersensitive and easily moved to tears; disassociation; panic attacks; a sense of isolation; lack of concentration. But they can also include self-destructive tendencies – like overspending. You live the high life. You rationalise that you'd been so close to death that you might and well live fast. And damn the consequences.

I travelled to Australia to recover immediately after leaving Iraq in April 2003.

I'd covered the Sydney Olympics a few years earlier and thought it would be the perfect place to unwind after the nightmare of war. But although I may have physically left Iraq, I was soon to find out that Baghdad wasn't so keen on leaving me. I slept badly, initially through jet lag, but soon the hours of darkness were joined by images of war and the tragic events of 8 April playing back like a horror movie in my head. My mind raced, every detail being cross-examined by an internal judge and jury. Had I done enough to get to the wounded and dying?

If I had gone straight upstairs, instead of the relative safety of the hotel basement, would I have made a difference? Were the decisions I made on that day grounded in my own fear.

The verdict was an overwhelming guilt. And now, here I was in Australia, far from the sights and smells of Baghdad. Safe in a hotel room, overlooking a beach in Surfers Paradise while others were still risking their lives in Iraq.

I started going out to bars and nightclubs, never short of someone to talk to in the manic state I found myself mired in. I was drinking vodka and Red Bull till my heart pounded, pouring petrol on my bonfire of self-loathing, while externally being the life and gregarious soul of the party. Even the simple act of brushing my teeth took me back to Iraq, causing me to retch and vomit at the memory of catching the cleaner in my bathroom of the Palestine Hotel, casually using my electric toothbrush on her rotten teeth.

I criss-crossed the country, joining American singer Grant Lee Phillips on his Australian tour, taking concert photos and self-medicating with alcohol each night. In Adelaide, the genial host of the venue, Richard Tonkin, was keen to chat as he'd being reading my Baghdad diaries avidly after Grant had been graciously posting them on his website during the invasion. A bottle of absinthe was produced after the show, and I struggle to remember anything for days afterwards. There are some very blurry photos though.

Eventually I returned to the UK, but I sensed I was in no way ready for work, so I headed to La Manga in Spain and the Hyatt Resort. There were some familiar faces in the BA lounge at Heathrow, famous sportsmen and women also on their way to La Manga to compete in the television series *Superstars*. I chatted with those interested in how things had been in Iraq,

several having watched Sky News during the toppling of Saddam's statue outside the hotel. An event our team had covered
live from the ground with a wireless radio camera while every
other broadcaster was tethered to their roof positions next to
the satellite gear.

The radio camera was a recent technical innovation which
David Chater had utilised to its full potential, speaking live to
newly arrived American Marines taking up defensive positions
around the hotel. We'd win an award for our coverage later that
year at the New York Festival, but my mind was far from award
season at this juncture.

Even in La Manga there was no escape from Baghdad.
The hotel nightclub was filled with American pilots from the
aircraft carrier USS *Theodore Roosevelt*, heading stateside after
supporting the invasion of Iraq from the eastern Mediterranean.
I showed them the photos I'd taken from my hotel balcony during
the first nights of 'Shock and Awe', giving them an unexpected
first-hand battle damage assessment, which they rewarded me
with drinks from the bar and one of their Top Gun coins.

I then found compliant drinking partners in the house
band and various Superstars who weren't taking the competition as seriously as others. Next up, more familiar faces, as
the England football squad turned up for some warm weather
training between internationals. I'd spent time with the squad
during the World Cup in Japan and some of the players had
also been following the war closely on Sky News.

When I returned to the UK the mania was subsiding, replaced
by the reality of maxed out credit cards, including a huge
amount on my company credit card and the shame of knowing
I would struggle to repay these debts. I withdrew into myself
and was soon enveloped in the blackness of depression.

I resigned from Sky News a few months later, sold my house to repay the debts and headed back to Australia for a new job with only the cash I had in my pocket and a head full of crushing despair. It would take me two years to find myself again.

In 2006 I joined the Al Jazeera English Channel in Qatar. I had cherished my time in Australia, working with some fabulous people, but the lure of being back at the heart of world events with a new global 24 hours channel was just too tempting, despite the risks. It was a decision that would take me back to Iraq ten years later and to a reunion with that familiar foe, PTSD.

I lost my job at Al Jazeera in 2017. The months before that I had spent seeking medical help for the trauma I was suffering after Mosul and the breakdown of my marriage. The network sponsored my work visa and rules are rules, even if you are on medication for depression and PTSD. I had no other choice but to head back to Scotland and move into my brother's spare room in the Scottish Highlands, feeling lost and completely alone. I forlornly sent out my CV for various roles, but I felt unemployable.

Despair and self-loathing gnawed at my every waking moment, so I slept a lot to compensate.

After months of darkness, I began to emerge from my cocoon, taking long walks in the Cairngorms and investing in a mirrorless camera and lens to try and engage my brain. I'd always had an interest in photography and with time on my hands I finally wanted to master it. I travelled around Scotland initially, reconnecting with my homeland. I then started planning trips to the Arctic Circle chasing the Northern Lights, something I'd always wanted to witness.

Keeping myself busy with photography and travelling kept me occupied. The ability to connect with nature was great for my recovery but every trip through Edinburgh Airport had its own challenges. My train connection at Edinburgh Gateway station to the Highlands meant standing on a train platform with trains passing through at high speed. Still troubled, I had to resist the temptation to jump onto the tracks and I would back away as far as I could, sometimes physically holding on to a pipe or railing as an internal battle for my soul ensued.

Over time the urges subsided, and I eventually found a new job in Belfast, but I still wasn't myself.

The long-term effects of PTSD are subtle but debilitating in their own way. You learn to cope by numbing your feelings, shutting out the extremes of emotion, knowing that happiness is the yin to the yang of sadness, and I couldn't trust myself with either. Another symptom is short-term memory loss, where you forget facts like people's names the instant you've been introduced, as if in the act of suppressing emotional pain you lose your ability to process basic information. Not a good thing to deal with when you're in a technical field like me. I found myself relearning skills that used to be second nature by repetition and becoming ultra-methodical to avoid stress. But when you're hit by a bunch of new things simultaneously you can become overwhelmed, and bad things start to happen in your brain. The hot flush of trauma on your face as you experienced the past in the present.

You also feel shame for not being the person you were, trying to hide the symptoms from others, losing even more of yourself as a consequence. But one thing I have learned is to share what you're experiencing with colleagues, hoping that they'll understand.

Most try, some do, and others think that you're an imbecile, having never experienced trauma themselves. Of course, journalists aren't alone in suffering from the effects of trauma and PTSD.

The loss of a job, a loved one, long-term illness and the break-down of a relationship are just some of the triggers for mental illness. Health workers, the police and military face situations that can cause lasting harm to their psyche and can lead to PTSD. During my first year in Belfast, I would get up early and prowl the streets with my camera documenting my new home. The amount of homeless people I encountered was shocking after years in the affluent Gulf. I would buy them a coffee from Starbucks and get the barista to write their name on the cup before sitting down with them for a chat. The common thread of these conversations was some form of trauma that had initi-ated their path to sleeping rough. Some turned to drugs to mask the pain; with others it was alcohol and they universally felt abandoned by society as they struggled with their mental health. For me, society is defined by how we treat our most vulnerable, and it was obvious that homelessness was the most obvious sign that we'd failed.

There's still a stigma around mental health and PTSD but employers are now recognising that it can be just as debili-tating as a physical illness. At the BBC, we have Mental Health First Aiders, identified with special lanyards on their ID cards that we can talk to about our mental health if we're struggling. There's also a Mental Health Awareness Week where we're encouraged to discuss our experiences and what has helped us to recover and manage our symptoms. I'm better now, not 100 per cent, but better. I rarely drink alcohol, eat healthy and escape with my camera to the Mourne Mountains, surrounding myself with nature whenever I can.

My advice, for what it's worth, is not to suffer in silence.

It's been a tough couple of years for everyone during this pandemic and I'm sure we've all felt a bit vulnerable at times. Job uncertainty, fear of the disease, the vaccine, travel, and the prospect of long Covid for those who have caught the virus, all factors. If you see one of your friends, colleagues or family acting out of character, a simple "are you OK?" can start a conversation that might lead to the realisation that they're not okay and need some help.

No matter how alone you feel, how ashamed you feel or how low you feel, there is help available. Just look out for each other.

Resolve, resilience and a thick skin

Patricia Devlin

PATRICIA DEVLIN is a former Crime Correspondent with the *Sunday World* and Investigations Correspondent with the *Irish Daily Star*. She has been a journalist for more than 15 years.

"People said they hoped I'd have to bury my kids."

I kept reading the message over and over, trying to take in every single word. My stomach lurched, I felt like I was going to be sick. I sat down on my bed and again went over, word by word, what was appearing on my mobile phone.

"Don't go near your Granny's in Maghera, Trisha. You will watch your newborn get raped. COMBAT 18!"

It was October 2019 and I'd just been back at work for a few weeks after taking a short period off to spend time with my baby son. Being self-employed in journalism means that unfortunately, maternity leave can be difficult. However, working for a Sunday newspaper meant I had a little more flexibility than my colleagues working on the dailies. It was my third child so I was becoming a pro at juggling feeds with filing copy. What I wasn't becoming so much of a pro at was coping with the escalating harassment, intimidation and abuse I was receiving on social media.

As a female journalist working on the crime beat, I was well used to some unsavoury comments from unsavoury characters. Apparently, if you aren't ruffling someone's feathers, you just aren't doing your job right. I still remember the first story I penned which caused a bit of stir. It was 2007 and I was on work experience at the *County Derry Post*, a brand-new weekly newspaper with a tabloid style. I was an eager intern keen to chase up as many stories as I could, and so there were many vox pops, calls to local councillors and charity events. I loved it all, and I will never forget seeing my name in print for the first time.

It had been my dream to be a reporter since I was 16 and finally at 21, I was sitting in a real newsroom.

The downside was it was all happening right bang in the middle of a financial crash, which was having a detrimental impact on newspaper advertising revenue. So, I worried that although I was so close to achieving my dream, there was also the chance I may not get a job. I was a young mum; my daughter had just turned one and luckily, I was able to continue and finish my journalism training with a fantastic support network. Six months after she was born, I was diagnosed with a severe form of post-natal depression which required counselling and medication. When I walked through the doors of the *County Derry Post* office in Dungiven, I was still in the midst of battling it. Writing was hugely therapeutic for me however, and one thing I didn't struggle with was producing stories.

In 2013, I was offered a contract with the *Sunday Life* newspaper in Belfast. After just six months, the editor sent me on a job 6,000 miles away to cover what was one of the biggest stories of that year.

Michaella McCollum, a 20-year-old woman from Dungannon in County Tyrone, had been arrested in Peru with another woman in an international drug trafficking probe.

Michaella, and her accomplice Melissa Reid, were found to be carrying more than £1.5million of cocaine in their suitcases. The women told police they had been kidnapped from the Spanish party isle of Ibiza, where they had been working, and held as hostages before being forced to travel to Peru to traffic the drugs.

In the days before her arrest, her worried family back home in Tyrone had launched a missing person's appeal after she failed to make contact. The appeal, which was backed by a number of Irish celebrities, eventually reached Peruvian authorities, who were more than happy to let the press here know that the up and coming model was safe and well – in jail.

Four months later, I was sitting across a table from her inside the exercise yard of the notorious Virgen de Fatima prison in Lima, and she was telling me her story.

Two days later, she was sentenced to six years and eight months in prison after pleading guilty to smuggling charges. And I was there to watch it all unfold. It was my first proper scoop. No one had spoken to this unlikely criminal who had made headlines around the world. I couldn't believe my luck when, for three and a half hours, she pored over every detail and answered any question thrown at her. Whether she answered those truthfully, was another matter. That story brought about my first real experience of trolling.

I was accused on social media of making a cocaine smuggler a celebrity, of "glamorising" drugs and "gutter journalism". Did the comments hurt me? Yes, very much so.

What probably upset me the most was that one of the most shaken tweeters, a seasoned reporter who worked through the Troubles, declared he would never buy the newspaper again. A bit extreme, I thought, especially given the fact that at the time of his dramatic pledge, the story hadn't actually been published.

But this was a peer, someone who would at the very least tip his hat to a local journalist who flew halfway across the world, gained access to a dangerous prison and landed a first ever interview with one of the most talked-about women in the North.

Perhaps he was right? He wasn't. The very next day, copies of the paper flew off the shelves; and again the week after that, when the second instalment of Michaella's interview was published.

Who wouldn't want to know how a young woman from a small County Tyrone town was set to spend her 21st birthday in a rat-infested Peruvian prison with little to no sanitation?

The best wordsmith in the world couldn't make that appear glamorous.

As Twitter and Facebook began to boom, so too did online hate and abuse.

You name it, I've been called it. I've been abused about my looks, my weight, my religion, my name. I've been sexually harassed on countless occasions and regularly sent pornographic pictures and messages from men.

In 2013, I was forced to go to the police about an individual who had been bombarding me with messages, not just on social media, but via email and telephone. Each time I'd block his account, he set up another one.

After almost a year of ignoring it all, I reported it to the PSNI who issued him with a Police Information Notice (PIN), which banned him from making any sort of contact with me for 12 months. The final straw was when, using yet another fake account, he posed as a grieving mother who wanted to do a story about her loss, just to speak to me. Sick.

In 2015, I moved to Dublin and became the Investigations Correspondent for the *Irish Daily Star*. There's working

in a newspaper and then there's working for an Irish tabloid
newspaper – the craziest, most fast-paced and unpredictable
environment. I loved every minute of it.

The job focused heavily on writing about organised crime
and corruption. There were also the weird and wonderful stories
which captured more attention than hard-hitting exposés.

After discovering that a woman in Dublin was selling her
breast milk to fitness fanatics online for almost €32 a pint, I
arranged to buy some. The next day the office phone rang off
the hook for me to go on numerous radio stations north and
south to talk about the unusual enterprise. I still get asked
about that story.

Paramilitaries and their activities are sadly still a problem
in Northern Ireland – and will continue to be for a long time.

Following a murder in 2019, I began writing more in-depth
about the activities of one of these so-called paramilitary
groups. This criminal gang has been responsible for flooding
the streets with drugs, attacking vulnerable people in their
communities, and extorting money from genuine business
people. In short, they have a grip on entire areas solely because
they instil fear and terror into those living there. So, it should
not have come as a surprise that these criminals and their
cheerleaders would turn their attention to me when I began
shining a light on their activities.

It started off with the usual comments appearing online
– stories were false, misleading, untrue. Then it escalated to
personal abuse. I was called an "obsessive activist" for writing
about a smear campaign being carried out against the family
of a murdered man, who dared to publicly call out those
responsible for his brutal killing. Then it moved to relentless
misogynistic abuse. The type that was intended to belittle and
humiliate.

Most of this was being carried out on Twitter, a platform where comments would be very much visible to everyone. Almost all of the accounts were anonymous – some had been set up solely to send me abuse. It was quickly becoming apparent that this was not run of the mill trolls; it was an orchestrated campaign.

I received phone calls from community workers and other public figures, who told me one loyalist had requested that they post statements or tweets criticising stories I had written. Others were told to stop engaging with me on Twitter by senior members of this so-called loyalist paramilitary group.

At this stage I was heavily pregnant with my son, and the stress of the constant stream of abuse took its toll.

After yet another night of trolling, I was driving to cover a court case when I was involved in a car accident. Thankfully I was OK but it floored me for a week. I didn't let it stop me writing stories and I continued on, filing copy from my bed. These people wanted me to stop, but I was not going to let them win.

The campaign escalated to my personal details being posted on a number of social media pages and forums, everyone and anyone encouraged to troll me. They included a link to my personal Facebook page, which included photographs of my children. People said they hoped I'd have to bury my kids, that I should be attacked in the street.

One dangerous criminal, with over 200 convictions, who I'd written about previously referred to me as the murdered journalist Veronica Guerin with the words "bang bang".

I was told I had a target on my back, and was called everything from a "tramp" to a "whore". One woman even suggested I wrote about paramilitaries because I wanted to sleep with them. Her comment was liked multiple times. One troll account had been able to find out personal information about a family member, and gleefully posted it online. I decided at that point, for my own wellbeing and health of my unborn child, I had to come off social media.

I took a break, but instead of that time out providing me with some relief, I was instead filled with anxiety, something I still struggle with. I was worried about what was coming next, what lies would they post? Who else in my family will be the subjected to this venom?

My little boy came into the world on 7 June 2019. I was able to take a few months out and went back to filing stories on a regular basis around September. I was just getting into some sort of routine when on the morning of 28 October, I received a message request to my private Facebook account.

It came from a profile which was not friends with me on the platform. The sender threatened to rape my new-born son, signing off with the name of a neo-Nazi terror group. What was also disturbing was that, whoever sent it, knew quite a lot about my family background. My grandmother was mentioned because she was the one who brought me up. The only relief in that message was that the location of her house was completely wrong.

As I sat down on my bed, feeling physically sick, I looked over at my five-month-old in his bouncer and I just cried. How could anyone even think those despicable words let alone sit down, set up a fake Facebook profile and send them? Who could think it was OK to threaten an innocent child because they don't like what I've written? I wasn't going to allow these bullies to target me or my family any longer.

I got my children dressed, dropped them off to day care and drove straight to my local PSNI station and made a complaint.

Since then I've been visited twice by police to tell me my safety is in danger. I was told loyalists planned to attack me in my car; myself and colleagues were later told of a threat from another paramilitary group, which may include attempts to intimidate our family members. At present, I have over 400 accounts blocked on Facebook and Twitter.

For a long time, I listened to the advice from colleagues, family and friends.

"Ignore it. Don't block...that's what they want. We are crime journalists...we get shit," one female reporter informed me. I was told not to show any signs of weakness. But it is not weak to have a zero tolerance to bullies. After a while they soon get tired of setting up the fake accounts – well, most do.

Yes, I still get called names, but I don't see it anymore. Plus, I have a very thick skin now, something I am immensely grateful for. It's also hardened my resolve to do my job, and continue to do it well. I will continue to make formal complaints about any social media account which crosses the line.

I am held to account for everything I write, the same should apply to everyone using the internet. Online abuse, harassment and intimidation against journalists, in particular female reporters, has exploded in recent times. Part of the reason behind this rise, I believe, is there is simply no deterrent. We are living a world where technology and social media has become intrinsically linked in our day to day lives. So, why then is it, that an individual who posts abuse and threats online, is treated less seriously than an individual doing so face to face?

Matters of life and death

Henry McDonald

HENRY MCDONALD has been a journalist for 35 years, was the *Guardian*'s Ireland Correspondent for two decades and is an internationally renowned author and broadcaster. He is the Political Editor of the *Newsletter* in Belfast

"...cordite was still lingering inside as the dead and wounded were taken away"

One July afternoon in the year of the plague just after I had turned 55, I thought I heard echoes of the Troubles behind me. They were quickening footsteps as someone was moving ever closer to me in the rear along the narrow pathway between the side of Belfast's Victoria Centre and the wall overlooking the tunnel into the shopping mall's underground carpark.

Suddenly out of nowhere there was a subliminal near-paralytic fear that took hold of my body and I froze. I fished out my iPhone from the top left corner pocket of my jacket and pretended I was taking a call or reading a text. It was a ruse that allowed me to turn around to discover who exactly it was that was moving towards my back at such a gathering pace.

In these few furtive seconds I recognised this familiar primal need to stop and survey what was going on. In that instant I thought about how many times I had written about or had heard first-hand accounts of the way human beings – both in uniform and without – were hunted down from the back, targeted at very close range and shot from behind usually in the head. The sensation of feeling someone bearing down on you out of your line of sight is something innate to many who lived through and survived the Troubles. Not just journalists as the first-page recorders of history but police officers, soldiers, rival paramilitaries, ordinary civilians.

The individual who had been coming up at pace towards me from the back in fact turned out to be a pleasant-looking, smiling young Indian man, probably one of the many software engineers or IT workers who have moved from the sub-continent to Belfast in recent years in order to train in places like the nearby BT Tower by the River Lagan.

He was probably bouncing along in relief like the rest of us that the great shut down of hedonistic pleasures from late March was finally being eased. There was nothing menacing or threatening about this chap with a spring in his step. He just appeared as happy as we all were to be out and about in a normal city once more. Nonetheless I was relieved to see him pass me by and let that sensation of suddenly feeling that you are quarry elapse.

Why had I been so unsettled on that warm summer afternoon? What had propelled me backwards in time to much darker days on my way to my favourite hostelry in the city centre? The answer to those questions was contained within a gift carefully covered in cardboard and which I had lovingly opened up just a few days after my birthday. It was a present to myself that I had bought online after seeing it advertised on social media during lockdown: the 40th anniversary release of Closer, Joy Division's tragic masterpiece.

Closer is my favourite album of all time even though the LP presages the suicide of lead singer Ian Curtis; some of its tracks containing darkly prophetic lyrics about existence and death. The work is also unique in rock history as being the better second album even compared to Joy Division's brilliant debut Unknown Pleasures. And so through four decades the songs on Closer have haunted and fascinated me in equal measure.

Yet it wasn't those tunes that left with me a sense of nervous foreboding that week in July. It was the album cover itself which triggered a memory that I thought I had buried deep long ago. It was the image from a tomb that reminded me of the body of a man I had seen back in 1989 through the long lens of a photographer's camera.

The cover of Closer was derived from some art-house photographs taken from the Appiani family tomb at a cemetery in Genoa, Italy. The picture chosen by the band just weeks before Curtis died is the depiction of *The Lamentation of Christ in the Tomb* with Jesus' body laid out on a marble slab, his beard pointing sharply into the air while his long hair flows onto the stone. Surrounding him are three female mourners including his mother Mary, with one of the other women throwing herself on the ground to weep bitterly.

I had forgotten about this stunning black and white image for many years but when I saw it again just as I slipped the vinyl onto the record player's turntable I instantly remembered what it reminded me of: a murder. An innocent man slain by sectarian killers; a husband and a father cut down in his prime.

Over three and half decades as a journalist I have witnessed the aftermath of many murders, shootings and bombings in the Northern Ireland Troubles. The memories of these individual and at times mass atrocities have been fleeting and unfixed; the mosaic of memory contained only in brief remembered fragments of time. Only certain things can illuminate these jagged, broken pieces of Troubles-recall and blood is naturally one such element.

Blood suddenly squirting from a drip that was used to drench my body with chemicals to attack the tumour in my stomach brought back the eerie sight of blood-streaked mannikins in the shattered window of a clothing shop in Omagh's main street on that Saturday in August just under five months after the Belfast Agreement signalled the end of the conflict.

More blood now. Congealed russet-coloured splodges of blood on the Formica tops of pub tables, which were used as make-shift stretchers in the immediate aftermath of the blast to take the dead and wounded away from the centre of the bomb site. Or the slashes of blood on the walls of the little hospital in the outskirts of the Tyrone town where the most seriously injured were treated before being evacuated by military helicopters to larger hospitals in Belfast.

Smell is another powerful force that can light up those fragments of hazy memory.

After being invited by the Irish Defence Forces to a live firing exercise on the Glen of Imaal in County Wicklow, prior to a trip to the Irish battalion of the United Nations peacekeeping force in South Lebanon at the end of the 1990s, my nostrils were filled with the acrid aroma of gun smoke hanging in the air. I could taste it as much as I could breathe it in. Inhaling its acidic scent, I was instantly transported to those terrible scenes outside Sean Graham's bookmakers in February 1992. That unforgettable waft of cordite was still lingering inside as the dead and wounded were taken away in ambulances after the Ulster Defence Association (UDA) murderers had fled the scene. On a bright brittle autumn day in Wicklow the smell came first and then back emerged the sight of one of the dead,

an old friend of my father lying slaughtered on the floor of a
bookies up in Belfast seven years before.

The power of smell occasionally carries me back to other
moments in time covering war, murder, mutilation, intimidation – not only in Northern Ireland but further afield.

The odour of putrefaction reminds me of the aftermath of
Israeli shelling on the South Lebanese village of Brashit in the
late 1990s. I was lucky enough to have been able to flee to the
safety of the Irish UN bomb shelter during the bombardment,
unlike Brashit's residents that night. In the morning when we
emerged out of the underground bunker, blinking through
the harsh winter sunshine I noticed that there was only one
living thing outside besides the light blue helmeted soldiers of
the Irish battalion. Or rather it had been a living thing. While
mercifully no civilians had died overnight in that particular
attack, a mule lay dead; the poor creature sprawled out under
the shell-shattered remains of a mosque. I could make out a
crimson tear across its stomach out of which oozed blood and
greyish organs, the latter giving off a foul stench across the
centre of the village.

For some unknown reason the smell from the dead animal
hung stubbornly in my nostrils for several days and at one stage
inside a Beirut hotel, on the eve of my flight back to London, I
wretched and vomited imagining that that reek of rotting offal
had followed me all the way up to Lebanon's capital city.

Yet never did I imagine that an arthouse recreation of *The
Lamentation of Christ* would transport me back to a building
site on the northern edge of Belfast in 1989.

I had only been working for the *Irish News* for a few
months and already I was worn down by the grim daily grind
of murders, shootings, bombings, kneecappings and beatings.

The news desk had been alerted to reports of a fatal shooting in the Rathcoole district and alongside one of the staff photographers, I raced up the motorway by the Belfast lough shore to the murder scene.

We found the dead man lying out on his back on the site and from the view finder of the photographer's camera, I could make out that the victim was bearded and had long hair. Even in that first glimpse this tragic scene made me think of images I had seen of Christ in the tomb. My first thought was of a sculpture beneath the altar where I had served on a child. It too had depicted *The Lamentation of Christ*.

That night when I got home after writing a report up about this dreadful sectarian murder, I flicked through my albums stacked up against the wall beside an old record player in a flat up in University Street. When I eventually reached Closer, I fished it out of the rack of other LPs and stared at that photograph of Christ surrounded by his inconsolable mother and the other women who loved him.

It was 1989 and as an atheist I had long ago abandoned religious faith but I still couldn't get that iconic Catholic image and the parallel one in front of my eyes flickering in my brain, of an innocent man laid out instead on the ground of a Belfast building site, out of my head. It stayed there for a few days in my mind before other disturbing images and experiences of the conflict I was reporting on day in, day out still raging all around me rushed in and flushed it away.

How did we cope? I say 'we' because I was never alone. I was part of a tight-knit corps of the first witnesses of history. Sometimes we were on the scene of a shooting, or killing, even before the ambulances arrived or the security forces turned up. We saw what the reader, the listener, the viewer, the wider public

both at home and abroad, did not see or hear. Producer guide-
lines, editorial ethics but most importantly of all the imperative
not to compound the grief of victims' loved ones, filtered and
tempered the raw footage we were processing in our heads.
Most of us coped with alcohol. Copious amounts of alcohol
that helped us absorb the pressure, lubricate our conversations,
allowing us – sometimes – to talk about it and often simply just
push these experiences to the back of the mind.

As well as the boozing I coped by throwing myself enthusias-
tically into the Acid House and later Rave culture in the early
1990s. In Britain the urban legend goes that MDMA – more
popularly known as ecstasy – converted legions of football
hooligans to the love drug culture of the Acid House scene and
away from a life of violence in soccer stadia and on the streets.
In Northern Ireland the dance culture fuelled by 'E' really did
create a kind of second post-Punk cross-sectarian youth cult.
Raves brought together a new wave of young people from
different backgrounds, united by their love of dance and the
drug associated with it. What I found out, however, in 1990-91
was that some of those dealing the love drug were using it to
fund their wars. As with many things in Northern Ireland the
moral universe gets turned upside down. The love drug became
the war drug.

So, I exited the scene when I discovered that both republican
splinter group the Irish People's Liberation Organisation and
several factions of the Ulster Defence Association – including
the notorious 'C Company' from Belfast's Lower Shankill area
– were importing and distributing MDMA from the Nether-
lands. It was not only morally dubious given that these groups
were filling their war chests with E-cash but also potentially
dangerous for a hack who trod on their feet from time to time.

The over-consumption of drink and the dance scene in turn of course led to physical and mental problems further on in life. In terms of mental health issues collectively, I stand to be contradicted here in stating that I know no one of the first and the second-generation veterans of Troubles-reporting who was ever open about seeking professional therapy or counselling. Maybe they did. If not maybe they, no we, should do so now.

Of course, in matters of life and death, perspective can be a vital antidote. It is important when we talk about the trauma-inducing Troubles to frame that conflict in the context of the other outright civil wars of the 20th century, or even perhaps just one single day in the life of the world wars over the last 100 plus years.

For example, in Lebanon, where I reported from in the early 1990s and frequently returned to up to 2000, the country endured a civil war that lasted for a decade less than Northern Ireland's Troubles. Between its outbreak in 1975 to its effective end in 1990 – ignoring those killed between that endpoint and the Israeli withdrawal around 2000 – approximately 120,000 people in Lebanon lost their lives.

In an even shorter conflict on the European continent, less than four hours by plane from London, more than 100,000 were killed. Bosnia's agony began in 1992 and ended three years later with a casualty rate the highest in Europe since World War Two.

At present, I am writing my third novel, part of which fictionalises the story of my great-grandfather Samuel who fought and survived the Battle of the Somme in 1916. On the first day of that offensive – 1 July – Samuel's 36th Ulster Division alone lost 1,856 men on that single corner of the Western Front. In less than 24 hours that carnage alone represents more than half of all the fatalities of the future Troubles.

My paternal grandfather Henry died in a German U-Boat attack near Cape Clear off the southern tip of Greenland in the Second World War. Two years before he perished in the Battle of the Atlantic, Henry's home city of Belfast was pulverised in two days over April and May by the Lufwaffe. In those two attacks during the Belfast Blitz nearly 1,200 of its citizens and some of their defenders were killed in the bombings, which apart from London was the greatest loss of life in German air raids on the entire UK.

None of these history lessons above, it has to be stressed, are in any way to minimise the deep sense of loss, bereavement and traumatic legacy that the Troubles have left all of us with. They do, however, on a personal level help me filter my own trauma memories, some of them burrowed deep into the subconscious, through the prism of perspective. In a real sense they enable me to cope better with what I saw, absorbed, reported on and later in some cases have been haunted by. Personally, whenever there are flashbacks or dreams of the Troubles past, I think about grandfather Henry or great grandfather Samuel and the sacrifices and privations of them and their generation. I suppose in a way this is the secular version of a non-believer praying for strength and succour to their favourite saint.

One of the most disturbing periods of my career covering the conflict occurred when my late cousin, journalist and novelist Jack Holland, and I were writing our book on the Irish National Liberation Army, *Deadly Divisions*. We came through that experience despite several death threats and dangerous physical encounters with three of the organisation's leading figures of the early 1990s, all dead now due to vicious inter-factional fighting. I can still remember one of these men invading my personal space in a very truculent, threatening manner one

Saturday morning inside Bewley's now defunct café in Belfast's Rosemary Street.

Nervous already about this meeting, arranged with the leaders of this faction of the terror group, I had asked to be excused at the start of our conversation so I could use the toilet. About two minutes later as I stood at the urinal, I felt a hand on my back pushing my face up against the toilet wall while another hand started patting both of my legs. When I protested and asked what the hell was going on my interrogator replied that he was searching for a wire. For a split second I thought that this was a way of calming me down before he produced a weapon and held it against my body. Or worse still started firing it. No gun was drawn, though. Only a few words of warning were muttered so I guessed that this body search was really designed to intimidate as part of a strategy to influence what I might write about him and his chums. There was, by the way, no wire or hidden microphone; only a small notebook the size of which fitted the palm of my hand, which I showed the trio when we sat down for coffee and buns.

Relations between us started to thaw over Custards and German Biscuits, and we agreed to meet again this time the following week with Jack coming along as well. Nonetheless, the earlier intrusive stop and search and the initial belli-cose tone of my interviewees reminded me of how volatile and exposed was this situation that I had found myself in on that Saturday morning in 1994. There were so many similar menacing encounters like this through the years that I have lost count of them.

Sadly, Jack succumbed to cancer in 2004; that terrible leveller which I had to battle with myself 14 years after we lost him far, far too soon. Reflecting back on that strange echo-filled summer of the first lockdown and that momentary Troubles flashback, a line comes to mind from Jack's superb novel about Ancient Rome and the Roman occupation of Britain. At the opening of *Druid Time*, his narrator, the governor of Britain, reflects back on his time as an imperial overlord and his entanglement with a perilous plot to steal Druid gold involving the increasingly mad Emperor Nero.

Marked for life by the horrors of the occupation and the murderous scheming back in Rome, Jack's narrator states: "I am Gaius Suetonius Paulinus and I have not been sleeping well lately."

Perhaps it might be something to do with the pandemic and those near total sleepless nights since the end of March 2020 but in these days of the plague when thoughts of mortality invade your consciousness, I now know exactly how Jack's Roman narrator must have felt.

I have given my soul over to what I do

Cathal McNaughton

CATHAL MCNAUGHTON is a Pulitzer Prize winning photographer and former chief photographer in India for Reuters – interviewed by Leona O'Neill

"There is a price to pay for what we're doing."

Even though I was brought up in the Glens of Antrim and people think you're away from all the Troubles down there, in retrospect, it has affected every single person that lives here. The Troubles weren't just in Belfast or south Armagh. The ripple effect impacted everyone. Even just coming from a nationalist community, we would be wary even going to hurling matches, of going through Protestant areas. The driver would have to do a long detour. You couldn't wear your Gaelic Athletic Association (GAA) top in Ballymena in case you were identified as being a Catholic.

Then there were the checkpoints. I remember soldiers patrolling the odd time. We never went to Belfast unless we were going to a GAA match, because my Dad was always wary of getting caught up in a roadblock or trouble. He worked in Belfast and got his fill of it every day and just didn't want to put us in that sort of danger. Unnecessary travel wasn't really a thing in those days. You would have been scared you would come across something or be part of something you didn't need to.

Growing up I remember there was a car bomb not far from my house. It was a booby-trap bomb that blew up a passing police patrol. My father and his brother were in the Order of Malta and they were two of the first responders. They had to deal with the aftermath of this IRA bomb. The Troubles were always there; they were always in the background, so much so that it became the norm. And that abnormal normal just follows you throughout the rest of your life. And very much so in the career that we in the media have chosen to do.

I started working in the *Irish News* in Belfast when I was 16 years old with Brendan Murphy, a veteran photographer who captured many of the iconic images of the Troubles. I moved from the Glens, where there wasn't a lot of violence, to Belfast and joined a newsroom whose staff reported on trouble and trauma every single day.

I started witnessing these things up close from a very early age and that became the norm to me. Because I was young, there was a certain naivety and there was an excitement that came from it. I suppose I got a bit of a rush from it. But what you don't realise is that it is the beginning of a path that you are on and you are going to have to pay that debt somewhere along the line. It all started then. I never considered the future impact of this work or what its cumulative effect might be.

I didn't go into journalism at the very start because I wanted to make a difference. I did it because I didn't like school and a friend of the family offered me a chance to go and see what it was like to be a photographer. Of course, that greatly changed over the years. I was very lucky because I fell in love with photography almost immediately.

I started at the tail end of the Troubles, but a riot is a riot no matter when it happens. A murder scene is still a murder scene. It doesn't matter when it happened in history. I saw riots and various sectarian murders. There was a lot of score settling towards the end of the Troubles. I remember the Lower Shankill Road was quite a hotspot at the time because of the loyalist paramilitary Johnny Adair and his cronies. And there was the Omagh bomb of August 1998 where 29 people and unborn twins lost their lives when dissident republicans planted a large car bomb. There was no shortage of traumatic events and the hostility surrounding them, trouble and conflict to cover when I was starting my career.

In the beginning, I enjoyed the work and found it extremely exciting. People might not like to hear that. But a lot of journalists and photographers stay in the profession because they do find it terribly exciting. There is a big adrenaline rush. And, of course, you're doing good as well. At the start, there is a real buzz, and I think that is why we put up with all that we do. Because I don't think you could do this job unless you really love it.

I think the kernel of the problem of journalists and PTSD is that we think that there is a hierarchy of grief or trauma. And how can I say that something has impacted me when someone else has been to Syria and they are not saying it has affected them? It's almost like we say to ourselves, there's no way that I can be affected by something because I haven't seen something as bad as someone else. And that is absolute nonsense. Everyone has their own threshold and the smallest thing can trigger someone and it can be a larger thing that can trigger someone else. I'm always wary sharing particular stories saying that this affected me, or that one. Because every single one of them has affected us, whether you know it or not, but there are some that stick out in your mind. I don't think that any one thing has affected me more than any others. There can be any number of individual moments that can impact on you. It can be just one small thing that can trigger a series of emotions or reactions. Any number of them that could be the straw that broke the camel's back.

I have seen a lot of disturbing things. It's not even necessarily things that I have seen, it's how I've reacted to things I've seen because you almost have to put emotions to the side. And so how you are dealing with trauma and grief that you are witnessing isn't very healthy. Because rather than facing it head on, you're compartmentalising it somewhere. We don't realise then that some day you have to deal with it.

Covering the genocide of the Rohingya in Myanmar had a significant impact on my mental health. In 2017, I was sent to Cox's Bazar in Bangladesh to cover the influx of displaced Muslims fleeing what amounted to genocide.

There wasn't any particular incident that impacted me but rather many. I found it difficult to watch hundreds of thousands of displaced people fleeing for their lives every single day. Every one of them had a terrible story to tell. Everyone had witnessed something terrible. When you are there trying to document that, a lot of that grief can transfer onto you.

I had been there two or three days. And I felt that there was something really unsettling. I just couldn't put my finger on it. There was something weird about it, apart from the fact that there were hundreds of thousands of people fleeing a regime. And I discovered that it was that there was no sound. It was very, very quiet. There was no laughter. You had tens of thousands of children. There were no children playing. None of them were laughing. There wasn't anyone smiling, ever.

When I would go back to the place that I was staying every night it really started to hit home. It was just so unsettling being surrounded by thousands of people and there is very little noise apart from the screams and shouts from people trying to get aid, who were basically fighting for their lives.

There are little things that stick with you. I remember being in the camps, taking photographs. It was during monsoon season. I was standing outside in a torrential downpour and a family came out of this makeshift hut and ushered me to come in out of the rain. It was a hut made from trees, branches and tarpaulin. There was nothing else to it.

I thanked them and told them that I was OK, I didn't want to invade their privacy, that they had enough going on and didn't need to be worrying about me getting wet. But they insisted that I came in. Inside there was absolutely nothing. They had a couple of metal bowls that they used for cooking and washing. In the hut they had one tree stump and that was the only thing that provided any sort of protection from the wet ground. And they insisted that I sat on the tree stump. And they all stood around and looked at me, because I was a foreigner, a strange looking person. I stood there until the shower passed, with them all looking at me.

All they had in the world for comfort was that tree stump. I recall just standing there thinking about all the material things I had. I thought about my life, which is in reasonably good shape, my family are all OK. And here are these people, who have absolutely nothing, they have got no future, God only knows what has happened to them in the past, and there they were letting me sit on this tree stump, the only thing in the world that they had.

That incident had a profound effect on me. It is something that I keep going back to. And it's something that I keep going over and over in my mind. Even more so than some of the terrible atrocities that I've seen. That simple act of kindness had the biggest impact on me rather than an act of violence.

At the start when I arrived in Cox's Bazar the aid situation was chaotic. There was no one overseeing it or controlling the distribution of aid. Random people, well-meaning people, charities, do-gooders, just arrived in lorries and distributed whatever they had. It wasn't controlled or managed so it was extremely chaotic and dangerous. People had nothing so they would literally fight for everything, not knowing what it is, because they have nothing to start with. It was like hell on earth. You had children fighting with adults, women fighting with children, men fighting with women. Humanity and all the rules and laws just broke down.

I remember at one stage myself and another photographer from *Associated Press* – because it was so chaotic on the ground – we were in the back of one of these lorries, shooting down. It was the only way we could take photographs without getting trampled. We had to put our cameras down on a number of occasions and take control of the distribution of the aid. Not because we are great people, but because we just had to. Some things are just more important than getting the picture or the story.

I remember seeing this one guy in the middle of the crowd and he was pulling some crazy faces, almost Goyaesque, the pain really coming out in his expressions. I was keeping an eye on him and he disappeared from sight. In this seething mass below me I spotted that he had actually fallen to the ground. These people were standing in seven inches of mud and excrement and whatever else. And this guy was getting trampled to death in amongst the crowd. I started screaming at the crowd – I didn't speak their language – to try to get this guy back up and out. But no one was paying any attention, because they were worried about themselves. They were worried about their own lives.

I managed to get some people to drag the guy out and underneath the lorry so that he was in some kind of safety. I jumped down to look at him. He was dying. I didn't know what was happening with him. Through lots of screaming and my Irish temper and gesticulation, I managed to indicate to a couple of men that I would give them money if they were to carry this guy over to one of the aid tents. This was Cathal McNaughton and not Cathal McNaughton the photographer.

We managed to get him over to an aid tent, who turned him away. They said there was nothing they could do. That was absolutely amazing to me. I managed to get them to carry him to my car which was nearby and we got him into the back and took off for the Médecins Sans Frontières field hospital where they took him in and treated him. I left then. I did my bit. I went back to my job.

This incident had an effect on me. While that was happening, I was taking photographs of the whole thing. So, I photographed that entire process from beginning to end, even when he was in the car, even when he was getting trampled, even when they were taking him out from under the lorry, even though I was helping that guy I was still doing my job at the same time. And that made me reflect on myself and what had I become – that I possibly saved this guy, but I am still taking the photographs as well.

You have these little things to deal with in the quiet moments that make you reflect.

I remember driving to Cox's Bazar one day. It was a single lane road. It was bumper to bumper, chaotic. It's a jungle road basically. There were thousands of people standing along the road. They weren't waiting; they just had nowhere to go. Because I was white and privileged and whatever, I suppose I just looked different. People would stare at me the whole time. And they would ask for stuff the whole time, which again, is understandable.

This was every day. After this went on for a while, I think I reached a limit. I remember I was sitting in the car in a traffic jam one morning and the car was surrounded by children. They weren't asking for anything. They were just staring in the window. Their faces were right in against the window just staring in. Staring intensely at me. Not in a playful way. Their faces were so very haunted. Again, because some of them were quite emaciated, there was this Goyaesque look to them. They were just staring. Maybe one of them would just slightly tap on the window, out of nervousness or whatever. They were just staring and staring with this really haunted look in their eyes. And they were everywhere I looked.

I remember this happening and I just couldn't take it anymore. I have a bit of an outburst where I wound down the window and I shouted at all these children to get away, to stop staring at me. And I think that was just a culmination of lots of things happening, not just at Cox's Bazar, but at other times. But I think that was just me reaching my limit.

I remember within seconds thinking, what the actual fuck am I doing? I have a child at home the same age as these children and here I am shouting at them, these children who have nothing. There are constant plays on your emotions and that can be quite hard to deal with over the years.

It's not like you can deal with every single thing you see, because you wouldn't be able to do your job otherwise. And that's why not everyone is suited to doing this job. It's a job that I love, and I don't regret any of it. But there is a price to pay for what we're doing and what we're seeing. Unfortunately, some people don't realise that and they don't confront the issues and it can lead to complications in their life.

The way I work, it's very important for me to connect with people emotionally because I think that shows in my photographs. I think that it's important to have empathy with your subject, so I have always tried to keep not too much of an emotional barrier because I think then things become robotic and lifeless. And you're not doing people's stories justice.

I think it's necessary to have some sort of a barrier, but I have given over my soul to what I do. I see the responsibility that I have and over the years I have realised how important and big that responsibility is. Maybe in the beginning I didn't, because it was just all about the adrenaline and the buzz. But then you realise the importance of your job and your vocation. People are opening up to you and showing the most intimate parts of their lives and the most intimate times. For you not to be empathetic, or not show some sort of respect, then I think you need to look at yourself as a person, not as a journalist. Ask yourself how you could do that. Because it's wrong on every single level.

Of course, you can't take every single thing on board every single time, but I just keep going back to the question, what would my mother think if she saw me behaving in this way? I have to be able to close my eyes at night and be at some sort of peace. It can be a very fragile peace. But generally, I can look back on my career so far and I am happy with how I have reacted towards people and acted with them.

You need to have your own moral compass. There is no definitive way for one person to act, because everyone has their own codes of conduct, their own levels of morality. It's all a very grey area. No one should tell you one particular way to cover a story, because everyone would do it differently. Maybe to get the information you need, you have to push people harder than you would like to. And it's important that you ask unsettling questions, and the questions that no one else wants to ask. You have to come to terms with that too. At times you have to be the person poking the tiger, because no one else will do it.

At times it's a very uneasy relationship, trying to be a good person and trying to be a journalist. Because they can fight against one another and quite often they are diametrically opposed.

A few years ago, I covered the conflict in Kashmir. The Indian government did not like that. I was on my way back to India after collecting the Pulitzer Prize in New York for my work in Myanmar in 2018. I was stopped at Passport Control and ended up back on the same flight I arrived on, straight back to Toronto. I never again stepped foot in India. My girl-friend was still in India, my apartment, all my belongings. Every single thing I had. All my cameras, all my friends, my job and my life was in India and I was never allowed back.

For a long time they wouldn't tell me what happened, but through government back channels I found that it was because of my work in Kashmir. The Indian government released a statement saying that I had breached the terms of my visa, which was nonsense.

I am not allowed to go back to India. But I am quite proud that by highlighting what was happening in Kashmir, at least it made a government take notice. It makes me happy and proud of the work I had been doing.

Coming home I was on an almost forced sabbatical. It wasn't something I had planned. I had been on this rollercoaster since I was 16 years old and all of a sudden I was kicked off it. I wasn't ready to get off. So that was a very difficult thing to deal with. I was forced to deal with stuff. My body and my brain decided that there were things that had to be dealt with and we are going to deal with them now. It kind of made the decision for me. And I have had to deal with all that over the last couple of years.

I am actually quite grateful that it did happen. It has made me re-evaluate my life and what is important to me. In my opinion, to do this job well, as a photojournalist, you have to be selfish, you have to make sacrifices, and you have to put relationships on hold. You have to put your work before everything. Whenever a big story breaks, you will want to go.

But you realise, when you're kicked off the rollercoaster, that nothing should be more important than family and relationships and friends. Family is the most important thing. And I was forced to confront that and indeed the selfish side of me, and take a look at myself in the mirror and ask, is this the type of person you really want to be?

It's like a Jekyll and Hyde situation. You want to be this good person, but you want to do this job and you are constantly fighting with yourself, saying that the job is for the greater good. This is how I am going to make an impact for humanity, or whatever way you want to sell it to yourself. And then the other side is, do I want to be a better father, son or husband? Not even a better one, but a good one, a present one. It's a difficult balancing act. It's an uncomfortable balance. I'm sure there are people out there who have found that balance, but I haven't been able to find it yet.

I did seek counselling in a peer network and in that I started to see problems and how to deal with them. I've learned that talking and sharing with others can actually help deal with these things. I was hearing about other media workers, a photographer in Jerusalem had some issue, another one in Syria had another issue and you start to think, that's kind of similar to what happened to me and how I felt. And then everyone shares their problems, and we try to deal with them, individually and collectively also.

I found that it is so important to talk to people about what is happening. And generally, I find that you can only really talk properly about what is happening to other journalists and photographers because they are really the only people who understand what you are going through.

I'm not sure you can do this job we do without paying some sort of a price. We are not robots. I don't think there is some remedy or elixir that will prevent you from feeling it in some way, either psychologically or emotionally. But you can lessen the effects of that by being more open about how you are feeling and being more open with yourself about how you're feeling.

I've been in some of the most horrendous situations imaginable but talking about it and saying that it affected you doesn't make you any less of a person. I think it makes you a stronger person because it helps you build stronger foundations for the rest of your career. You're building a very shaky foundation if you just ignore these things. If you ignore things, you are only ignoring them temporarily. Some things are imprinted on the hard drive of your soul somewhere and they are going to have to be dealt with. They don't disappear.

Talk about it. Talk to your colleagues. Talk to your friends. You don't have to sit down every day and analyse it. But just talk about it and how it made you feel.

There is absolutely no shame in being emotional about things you have seen. You're only human.

Burying your feelings can come back to bite you

Barbara McCann

BARBARA McCANN has more than 45 years experience as a broadcast journalist, working for ITN, UTV and the BBC – interviewed by Leona O'Neill

*"Images of the dead are never far
from my thoughts to this day."*

"Sheet! We're in a fucking minefield."

Tim Lambon's strong South African accent jolted me into consciousness. I had been sleeping fitfully in the rear passenger seat when our vehicle suddenly slammed to an abrupt halt. It was January 1991, and the Gulf War was about to enter its final phase. We were in the desert between Iraq and Kuwait, surrounded by landmines.

Tim had been in the military and his experience had heightened his awareness of danger and his ability at getting out of it. I trusted him with my life. We were both accredited war correspondents but, a day earlier, we had defied orders to remain within sight of the Allied Forces and their PR machine.

We'd slipped away from the British television media pool's base in Saudi Arabia and crossed the desert alone, determined to see what was really going on in the conflict without the watchful eyes of the British and American military.

This was long before mobile phones. We couldn't tell anyone where to find us and now it felt like we were both about to die a horrible and painful death in a foreign country. I was fearful that my family and friends would never know what happened to me or know that I had loved them until the end.

The tension was etched on Tim's jawline as he silently and slowly inched the vehicle across the sand. It took two adrenaline-fuelled, survival-driven hours for us to get clear but, always the reporter, I stuck my head out the window to take a photograph of a landmine that our vehicle's rear passenger wheel narrowly missed. I still have it, somewhere.

I slept little during my three months stint covering the first Gulf War for the national television broadcaster, TV-AM: I was only too aware that a mortar shell could explode beside us at any time. Towards the end of the coverage my nights were spent bivouacking next to an army tank or sleeping on the floor of a room of what was once a luxury hotel in Kuwait that had been destroyed by fleeing Iraqi soldiers.

There was no running water, no electricity and very little to eat. The elevators didn't work and after filing my reports via satellite link-up at the makeshift media base, we had to climb hundreds of stairs each day to the top floor of the hotel to get a room to sleep in. The hours were long and exhausting with little time off, especially when reporting from danger zones around the world. I suppose it was a natural progression from my experience reporting on the Troubles for broadcasters in Northern Ireland where I had grown up.

When people ask me how long I've been a journalist, I reply that I was born into the job. From no age, when the news was on the radio or television in our house my brother and three sisters and I had to be quiet while my parents tuned in.

My mother Margo had worked in the *Irish Times* and my late father, Brendan, was a multi-award-winning press photographer with the *Irish Independent*.

Dad grew up in a cottage in the grounds of Omagh Convent where his father was the gardener. Mum was from the Donegall Road in west Belfast, which was where we moved to in 1969, just months before the Troubles broke out. Some would judge it as bad timing, but west Belfast later provided a base for much of my reporting of the bombings and shootings.

As a reporter during the Troubles, there were many occasions when both my colleagues and myself found ourselves in the wrong place at the wrong time, caught up in the midst of danger. On one occasion in the late 80s, a riot had broken out in Belfast city centre. Stones and bottles were being directed at soldiers in full riot gear, who were responding by firing plastic baton rounds to disperse the rioters. I thought I was in a safe place standing far enough back from the danger against the shutters of a shop. There was a loud bang like the noise made from a gun firing a plastic baton round. It was. I actually saw the missile hit the wall of a shop and, in what appeared like slow motion, bounce once before hitting me on the shin bone. I hadn't been quick enough to jump out of the way. I was lucky: it hurt more than my brain initially registered and left a massive bruise on my lower leg but nothing worse.

I can't quite remember the date but there was an incident in the Bogside in Derry in 1988 or 89. Soldiers had shot a young man who it was claimed was a member of the IRA. I headed to the city with my three-man crew – Irwin, Terry and Alan – to report on it for TV-AM. There had been rioting on the streets following the shooting near Free Derry Corner and though by the time we arrived it had subsided, things were still very tense. In the darkness, people gathered in agitated groups, talking and shouting, wary of any strangers or TV crews around. There were quite a few reporters covering the story. I was about to do my piece to camera when I was grabbed by the arm by a young guy wearing a hoodie and his face covered with a scarf. I had no idea what was coming. I initially thought he wanted to show me something to film but when I looked again at what he was holding in his right hand, I realised he had a gun. I could be a bit mouthy in my early days as a reporter, standing up to the so-called 'hard men'. I realised early on that when faced down by a slip of a girl, most backed off. But that night in Derry I wasn't going to argue with the armed youth pulling me alongside him to an alleyway yards from where we'd been standing in the crowd. Only my soundman Terry was with me at that stage and he followed, as frightened as I was becoming. We'd somehow got separated from our cameraman Irwin and our driver Alan. The youth mumbled something about being in the IRA and ordered the two of us to sit on a low wall. He pressed the gun to the back of my head and told us not to move or he would shoot. We just sat there, frozen in terror, not speaking a word, looking straight ahead into the dark empty street. I remember thinking, not for the first time, I am going to die tonight. There was an eerie silence. There was no-one else around. It seemed like a lifetime but probably only a few minutes passed before I dared to whisper: "I think he's gone. I don't think he's coming back."

Terry's reply was barely audible: "Are you sure?"

My heart was thumping.

"Yes," I shouted, "run!"

Terry didn't need convincing and ran aimlessly with me until we got back to the crowds again. It took us about half an hour, but we managed to find the rest of our crew who had no idea what had happened to us. Within minutes we were speeding out of the city. In those days of no mobiles, there was a phone installed in the car and I telephoned the news-desk in London to say we had been threatened and were not going back. We had enough footage to cover the story and, to his credit, the editor's only concern was for our safety in the end.

I stared death in the face again when I was almost killed in a helicopter crash in Enniskillen in October 1996. My back was broken in the accident and both kneecaps were dislocated. I spent weeks in the hospital and months in a back brace.

I've got to tell you the worst thing you can ever hear your pilot say is "mayday mayday" before crashing.

I was on one of three helicopters taking journalists to cover a story in Enniskillen and one of four onboard, including the pilot, who were hospitalised.

The editor of the *Sunday World*, Jim McDowell, and Joe Kearney of the *Irish News* were the other two journalists on the helicopter – a five-seater Bell Jet Ranger.

By good fortune an RAF helicopter crew had been refu-elling nearby and on hearing the pilot's mayday distress call over their radio frequency flew directly to the crash scene and airlifted the first of the casualties to the Erne Hospital, which had gone into emergency mode.

The accident had been caused when a small locker door flew open at the rear of the helicopter when we were at a height of about 1,500 feet and a jacket which had been stored inside, wrapped around the rotor blade of the craft and sent it into a spiral.

I remember the immediate relief of surviving the crash but panicking as I was being stretchered into the RAF helicopter, afraid it too was going to crash. For years afterwards, I worked through the pain of my injuries but still suffered terrible nightmares. I now know that a traumatic incident, like the helicopter crash, can trigger flashbacks to other incidents.

Physical injuries have healed but emotional wounds are close to the surface. To this day I cannot watch anything about the Troubles or the Iraq war. I suppose it is a form of PTSD. Both UTV and BBC produced what I am told were outstanding programmes on the 50th anniversary of the conflict but I still couldn't watch. It was the same for the anniversary of the Lockerbie disaster, the Omagh bombing of 1998 and other programmes where I was personally involved in reporting at the time the incidents happened. I have witnessed a lot of death and grief and been scared many times in my 40-plus years as a journalist. I can feel other people's loss and because of it, I have learned to block out all the horrendous and terrible sights. But that has a price: burying your feelings and not talking about them, no matter how well you think you are doing, can come back to bite you at the most unexpected of times.

I am too sensitive to other people's sorrow or grief. Throughout my career, every time I arrived at the scene of an atrocity or fatal crash, I have first always said a private prayer for the dead or dying. It has never mattered to me what religious or political views they held. They all had someone who loved them.

Images of the dead are never far from my thoughts to this day: the group of Iraqi soldiers standing like statues on the back of the army truck, their life sucked out of them by a fuel-air bomb; the lifeless recruit sitting upright in another vehicle touching his wedding ring; the mutilated bodies of the victims of the Lockerbie bombing lying in the fields around the town; the grief on the faces of the family of Shankill Butcher victim Joe Donegan when the RUC officer brought his watch to them to identify when his body was found.

Saying a prayer at the scene as a working journalist has been my way of dealing with the sadness and helping the victim. The passage of time has made details a little hazy, but no matter how many years have gone by, I have always remembered the person in the story.

Every day is a lesson

Niall Carson

NIALL CARSON has been a press photographer for 25 years, working for newspapers and agencies in Belfast and Dublin – interviewed by Leona O'Neill

"I started shouting: 'I've been shot! I've been shot!'"

I grew up in Andersonstown in west Belfast. One of my very first memories as a four-year-old was of the 1981 Hunger Strikes and Bobby Sands' death and funeral. My family lived in the South Link Flats, a place that overlooked the site where the two British Army corporals – Derek Wood and David Howes – were killed during an IRA funeral after inadvertently driving into the cortege. It is a notorious place.

Down there, there's a place called 'Aggro Entry'. Basically, it's two shops with a narrow alleyway between them. Police or army vehicles that drove through it just got everything thrown at them and on top of them. I can remember being very young, looking out the window and seeing people throwing petrol bombs on top of Saracens. I remember seeing a soldier on fire, running. I wasn't frightened by the sight; I was more fascinated. I didn't sense any danger from it or felt any shock. It was just something very extraordinary to see. I think that seeing those types of sights as a child gave me some kind of armour for the job I did when I grew up.

My parents would always watch the news, as everyone did in those days, so I was kind of exposed to it. They were very political people. They were big Sinn Fein people too and they were always marching in the political rallies. As a child I happened to be there on the day Sean Downes died at a protest after being hit by a plastic bullet fired by the RUC. I was maybe seven or eight years old and had been brought along by my parents. It wasn't a rally that they had expected to turn violent.

I have another really horrible memory from my primary school days. I went to St Oliver Plunkett Primary School, and we had a little allotment at the back of the school. I used to potter around in there, looking at the flowers and the plants. There was someone shot dead in the alleyway right beside it one night. I have this memory of a guy in a forensic suit, using little plastic tweezers to pick fragments of skull and brains off the plants in the school allotment and I'm standing there looking at him. I don't remember being told to stay away from it, but it was the same thing again. I wasn't appalled by it, more fascinated. I think it was because it was a day and daily occurrence, hearing about death and also you would have heard explosions thundering around different parts of Belfast on a daily basis. I never felt any danger.

My parents were very strict about riots. They wouldn't let us anywhere near them. But I was always very curious. One day there was a bus burning at the top of my road and I thought I would go up and have a look at it. It was quite exciting. The bus was just a wall of flames and I couldn't see the other side of it. But there was a crowd of people behind it, and they were throwing rubbish into the bus to keep it ablaze. Then someone threw a brick at the bus from the other side, and it went right through the flames and smacked me right in the face. I was completely shocked; you don't expect a half brick to come flying out of a fire. I was only 10 years old and that was the last time that I ever went near a riot out of curiosity, until I started taking pictures. That incident really frightened me.

I started off in photography doing a workshop in Belfast Exposed when I was around 15 years old and then I started my apprenticeship aged 16 in the *Irish News*. That's obviously where I met the photographer Brendan Murphy, and I knew then that this was what I wanted to do.

It was while working there I took my first really powerful photograph. I was sent to a Protestant Black Preceptory march in Newtownbutler, a mainly Catholic village in County Fermanagh. There was really bad trouble at it, people were injured. It was just leading up to the Drumcree dispute. Things were really tense at parades.

In Newtownbutler there was a stand-off in the street. The police line had moved forward and a woman was knocked unconscious by a police baton. Her partner was really angry and ran at the police line by himself with his fists flying. So, I got this picture of one man standing against an entire row of riot police with his wife lying unconscious on the ground.

It was shocking but also very exhilarating. At that point the police didn't bother me or push me out of the way. They let me have a little leeway to be there. It was very thrilling to be that close to danger, but not actually be part of it.

I had a life-changing moment when I was in the *Irish News*. Because I lived in west Belfast I went the entire way through my life, until around 18 years old, without ever speaking to a Protestant, meeting a Protestant or being in a Protestant area. So, I was seeing the other side of the community through the prism of never having met them, hearing only what other people were saying about them, what my community thought of them and it wasn't very nice.

I covered an RUC man's funeral in 1997. The constable's name was David Johnston and he had been killed by the IRA. I was 18 and it was quite daunting. I have never before spoken to anyone in the RUC who wasn't in riot gear. I remember the man's young son was really, really distraught. He was there wearing a green shirt and waistcoat and he just reminded me of a little Catholic boy who was making his Confirmation. He was only around seven years old, and he was walking behind his father's coffin. He was totally distraught, really upset and I was very upset just being there and photographing it. It was my first time doing a big funeral like that. I have been to plenty of republican funerals, but they were more like showpiece events. They weren't really emotional funerals. Obviously for the relatives of the person lost it was emotional, but a lot of the people who were there were all there as a sort of show of strength. But at this funeral of the RUC man, everyone was emotional. The man was only 30 years old when he was killed.

That incident started to change my opinion of the police. Up to that point to me they were just uniforms. This was the first time that I was starting to see them as human beings and see the effects that the Troubles were having on the families. It was a big shock. For me up to that point the Troubles was all fire and petrol bombs and explosions. I had never really seen the real effects of someone who was murdered before. It was another moment that made me think this is a really privileged job we have. We're educating ourselves about life.

I don't even think I took a really good photograph that day. My mind really wasn't on what I was doing. I was still very young, and I felt like I was intruding on the grief of the family.

At the beginning of my career funerals for me were very, very difficult. I was quite religious at that point. I was a devout Catholic when I was 18 so I would find it difficult working at religious services, even photographs and inside churches and Masses and Protestant services. But a couple of thousand funerals later and you just do the job. You are just thinking about the shape of the picture and the space you have to fill in the newspaper while obviously trying to be as sensitive as possible to the people who are involved.

Holy Cross in 2001 is a really bad memory for me also. All of us thought that the Troubles were over. I thought I had missed all of that because I started the job at the very tail end of it in 1997, when everything started to settle down. I came in at the end of Drumcree and as a photographer I was kind of sad that I had missed the big points in the Troubles.

At the time of the Holy Cross dispute in north Belfast, when loyalist protesters tried to prevent Catholic schoolgirls going to their primary school, I was working for the *Andersonstown News*. To see adults shouting at little children, saying really despicable things to them, and to see children shouting sectarian slogans at each other, was really upsetting. There were people throwing bags of urine at the kids. There was all sorts of horrible stuff. It was very difficult to cover and try and not get emotional about it when you were there.

Around four years after that I was there when a blast bomb was thrown in Ardoyne. By that stage as a photographer I felt very confident. I had done a few riots and a fair few incidents. I had photographed confrontations with the police and the army. I thought I was OK. Indeed, I might have had notions that I was James Nachtwey, a very famous war photographer.

There was a lot of really serious trouble that day in north Belfast around an Orange Order march. The water cannon was out. There were police getting knocked down and ambulanced away. There were people getting baton charged. There was blood everywhere, broken glass and bottles. It was really quite exciting. I remember thinking to myself, this is great, this is what I'm in this job for.

I was photographing a policeman who had been injured. He was lying on the ground after dissident republicans had dropped a breeze block on his head from the shop roofs above. His colleagues were very worried about his neck. He was being very carefully put onto a back brace stretcher. They had taken his helmet off and were about to put a neck brace on him and this blast bomb just landed right beside him. His colleagues and the medics just hit the deck.

Meanwhile I was looking at it and couldn't make out what it was. To me it looked like a sock or something but there was smoke and sparks coming from it. I thought, that's definitely a bomb but I didn't get time to turn or run or anything. It just exploded right there, right in front of me. There was a huge bang, and I was deaf. I was looking around and I could see these police officers, straight back helping their colleague on the ground. I was amazed at how quickly they were back to it. I just kept clicking. I didn't turn or run away. I wasn't injured and I thought I was lucky. I just continued doing what I always did, taking pictures, deaf or not.

I might have been dazed, but I didn't realise how serious it had been until I saw the BBC's Chris Lindsay. He had been hit in the back by shrapnel and it looked like he had a really bad injury. There was blood pouring from his back through his shirt and I could see that he was in real agony. It was really frightening to see. I looked past him and saw another man lying on the ground, his leg was bleeding profusely.

I knew the two of them were standing behind me at the moment of the blast, because I had spoken to Chris earlier on. As I was looking at them in the aftermath of the blast, I wondered how they got hurt and I didn't because they were behind me. I think it was just luck that it went over my head or between my legs or somewhere, but the shrapnel didn't hit me even though I was standing right beside it.

It scared me, the sight of the two guys badly injured. I felt that if anyone threw another bomb over here there was nowhere for me to go. I had no personal protection equipment of any description on. I was wearing a t-shirt and jeans. As soon as I saw the pictures on the back of my camera, the reality started to sink in, and I needed to get out of there. I felt very lucky.

For a few days after that incident, I had terrible flashbacks. I could hear the sound of the blast and the smell of the gunpowder, or whatever was in the explosive device, lingered around me for what seemed like days. My mind pondered the 'what if' scenarios a fair few times.

Not long after that there was another riot in West Circular Road. There were loyalist gunmen on top of houses, and they were shooting at the police and the army. There was a blockade in the middle of the road. I was standing on top of an electric box trying to photograph over the top of the police jeeps. I suddenly heard bullets whistling past my head and hitting the tree right above me. The shredded leaves start falling down on top of me. I just jumped down and said: "No, that's me. I'm finished and I'm out of here." It was so close, and I was really frightened.

Another photographer, Crispin Rodwell, took a really good photograph from up the street that day. It was of soldiers looking terrified, they were shouting and there was rubble strewn everywhere. It was a really bad riot. I was very jealous when I saw the picture. But at the same time, I was too afraid; my previous experience from Ardoyne I think stopped me from going back up that street and I went home safe. But then I can say that fate eventually caught up with me in 2011.

I had been to the Short Strand a few times before. It's a nation-alist area in east Belfast, on a peaceline with loyalist streets on the other side, and there had been a stand-off between rival crowds. I was on the Catholic side at Clandeboye and there was a little Protestant enclave called Cluan Place over the wall.

I was down there in the middle of the night one night when there was trouble and a World War Two hand grenade was thrown over the wall and landed in amongst the media. It didn't explode, thankfully. It was one of those Mills bombs that looks like a pineapple. It just clunked on the ground at our feet without exploding. Everyone was just looking at it and taking photographs of it. It just didn't feel real or dangerous.

Fast-forward a few years and in 2011 I'm on the other side of the wall now, on the Newtownards Road. The police were sitting in their jeeps and there were about seven news crews watching the trouble from afar. Again, I was quite far from where the trouble actually was.

I had a really nagging feeling and I could hear people talking over the wall on the Catholic side. There were little gaps in the wall, and I was saying to the people on the other side of the wall, "Lads there are no loyalists here, it's just the media and the police, there's no one trying to get over that wall". I tried to put them at ease in case they were thinking there was some kind of incursion going to happen. But that shows naivety on my part, because they were obviously planning to attack the police; they knew that the police were there and that's who they were looking to shoot.

The media were all just standing around talking and out of the corner of my eye I saw someone on the top of the wall. I saw the blue surgical gloves and a Celtic scarf, a baseball cap down over the eyes and I knew that this guy had a gun. Me and another couple of the guys saw him at the same time and started shouting "Gun! Gun!" and we all turned to run away. I heard big bangs, around four maybe, and I felt this massive whack in the back of my thigh. My first thought was that the police had shot a plastic bullet at the gunman, and they had hit me by mistake. I just assumed that it was a plastic bullet because of the impact. It was a very, very strong force, like a punch to the back of my leg. I went to take a couple of steps and for some reason my leg just seized up and I couldn't put my foot on the ground. My muscles just pulled like an elastic band. I felt a strange sensation like cold liquid running down my trouser leg and I thought to myself, Jesus, I've been shot here.

I looked down and saw a hole in my jeans. The bullet went into the back of my thigh and straight out the front. I was thinking what the hell do I do here?

I just started shouting "I've been shot! I've been shot!" and everyone was just looking at me. I suppose they couldn't see any major bleeding or anything, but I knew. I couldn't get anyone to help me. I saw a policewoman in a van looking at me. I put my hand up like a kid in school trying to get the teacher's attention. I think I actually said, "Excuse me, I think I've been shot". Fair play to her, she got out of the jeep straight away with the first aid pack and the police drove a water cannon out into the middle of the street to block the street to give me some cover while she treated me.

I was really in shock. I started to get very cold and shaky. I got on my phone and called my boss and I phoned my Mum, just to let her know what had happened and to get her to contact my girlfriend. I was big into Twitter at the time and the photographers around me were joking that I was tweeting about it before I even got to the hospital.

I didn't know at that stage how badly injured I was, but I certainly had total trust in the policewoman, because I knew they were well trained. And I knew that once the ambulance came, I'd be in the Royal Victoria Hospital in five minutes. I knew that they had treated every type of Troubles-related injury in there also.

I knew there was a hole in my leg and there was a lot of blood, but I had an idea that they hadn't hit an artery. My leg wasn't totally drenched in blood and the policewoman didn't seem panicked, she was very professional, telling me all the things she was doing and that they were going to get me an ambulance.

I thought the ambulance would have been there in seconds, but it didn't come. I was put into the back of a police car and the senior police officer came over to see if I was OK. He asked if I had any pain and I said no, I was still in shock. I couldn't feel any pain whatsoever. He told me that they were going to get me out of there shortly but there was a bit of an issue with the ambulance. There was an ambulance depot just across the street. So, the police drove me there but the ambulance crews wouldn't come out because one of the bullets had struck their window or building and as far as they were concerned they were still under threat of being shot. This was all three or four minutes after the shooting happened. The police convinced them that it was safe, and the paramedics came out and, of course, they were absolutely brilliant. I was immediately put on a drip and they give me painkillers.

When I got to the Royal Victoria Hospital from the Short Strand, which is only a few minutes away, my mum and my sister were actually waiting in A&E for me. After I called them, they sped straight down the Falls Road. I suppose they didn't know what to expect, they just heard me saying I'd been shot. I could be dead, anything.

The doctor said I had to go straight to surgery. He said they had to do something to prevent infection. They basically had to scrape out a tunnel through the hole where the bullet went through, just to make sure that there were no threads from my clothes or any metal fragments from the bullet. They didn't stitch it up, but rather let it heal itself. It took three months for the hole to heal up.

There was someone else shot on the same night. His bone had been shattered. He was in traction for months and months, basically hanging upside down in some contraption in the hospital so the bones could grow back together again. It was a serious injury, and you would have trouble walking again after that.

While I was waiting for my surgery, I was remembering the many people who I had photographed in the hospital over the years after kneecappings, a form of punishment meted out by paramilitaries on both sides, when people are shot through the knees. I had seen some very gruesome injuries. I knew being shot in the leg was no picnic. I knew that if you're hit in the wrong place you can bleed out and die, or you could lose your leg. It was frightening, but I was just happy that it wasn't as serious as it could have been.

While it was all going on at night my photographer friend Colm Lenihan actually drove my car to the lock-up in the *Irish News* so all my gear was put away safely. That was a big relief for me. I had thousands of pounds worth of photography gear there and I was really worried about it.

I was very lucky to be in a staff job at PA when I was injured. I was compensated because they have a duty of care. They were absolutely fantastic with me. They told me I could take as much time as I need and if I had any medical costs whatsoever, they would pay them.

It was hard to get back out and cover that type of situation again, riots and the like. I can't remember the first riot after that, but it was up in Ardoyne where the blast bomb had gone off all those years before. I was definitely a lot more frightened. I would have been using longer lenses. I still got nice pictures of petrol bombs, flames and water cannons and very dramatic stuff, but from afar. I thought to myself is it really worth getting into the middle of that? I don't wear heavy protection gear, a flak jacket or a helmet, because at night when it's dark your silhouette could look like a policeman, and they are considered targets by some.

I was there the night Lyra McKee was shot dead while observing a riot in Derry. I had the hindsight of having some hostile environment training at that stage and I had also had the experience of standing beside a jeep and being shot, so I was using brick walls for cover and if I was looking out it was very quickly, taking a photo and back in. I wasn't standing in the middle of the road. I was hyper-vigilant. If you hear the crack of a gun – and it's an unmistakable sound – you get down and get behind a brick wall as quickly as you can.

At the time of the shooting, I was actually getting something out of my car and I came back and saw the absolute pandemonium with all the people there and the emotion in the people she was with. It was chaotic and no one knew what had happened. A lot of the crowd thought that the police had done something to her. The police, who were trying to get her into the jeep, were having to deal with a hostile crowd. I still wasn't sure but when I arrived. I thought someone was being arrested, just by the angry reaction of the crowd. It just shows you how out of control those situations can become.

After the police drove Lyra away, the scene became very eerie as they put the crime tape up. I assumed that there would be more shots and I was hugging walls and ducking down behind cars. Even the police who were putting up the crime scene tape had their hands on their holsters at all times. They were tense and expecting more shots.

It was pitch black and seeing the police with fear in their eyes, it was not a nice place to be.

Only the next morning we found out what had happened to Lyra, and the tragedy of her being so young with her whole life ahead of her. It was very upsetting. That night really got me thinking. I thought that could have been me on any of those occasions when I dodged bullets. Or on the night I was shot, I could have been shot in the head, like that poor girl. That is when I started to really think. I have been in that position where she was standing so many times. And the people who are shooting up the streets obviously don't have any consideration for bystanders. Why they did that I don't know.

I was a father at that stage and that was really playing on my mind. I think once you have children, you don't feel as invincible. Before children I suppose you think, if I got killed, I was a photographer doing his job. But now I think that I don't want to leave my little son without a Dad. I would feel very guilty if that ever happened. My son is only five and they are so vulnerable at that age. He would be absolutely devastated, his mother would be too, as well as my partner and my parents. So, you do think, as you get older, what is the risk and what is the reward? The more you have to lose, the less the reward seems to be. Whereas when you are younger it's all about making a name for yourself, get the front page of the paper and win the world press photo awards. Now, family comes first and coming home safe is what matters.

Beyond the violence, the one story that really traumatised me was the Buncrana Pier tragedy, when a family drowned after their car slid off a jetty and into the harbour in County

Donegal. I think maybe because I have a young son, I actually couldn't cover the funeral; I asked a colleague to go instead. I just couldn't do it. In the days leading up to the funeral we were in Buncrana and had spoken to the guy who had rescued the baby and also to eyewitnesses and I had played it all over in my mind. What would I have done? What did the man do? What did the family do? I was standing down at the pier and looking out to where the car would have been and just thinking that the sea was so calm. And in my mind, I was visualising the car slowly sinking and the panic and the shouting and the screaming.

It was a horrific thing, like something out of a horror movie, and I had nightmares about that for a long time. It was horrible and nobody could do anything about it. It was the helplessness of the children in the car and the man. That was one of the stories that was just so awful that I couldn't continue on with it. I wanted nothing more to do with it. I just couldn't physically do the funeral. I would have been too upset to see those children's coffins. It was just so sad. It was just one of the stories to really hit home. It was just an awful, awful tragedy.

I have covered a lot of tragedies, murders and court cases.

I was also beaten up at a funeral in Dublin. A drug dealer had been killed and another man had taken his own life in police custody. I made a real rookie mistake of driving into a cul-de-sac on my own. I was taking pictures out of the car window in an area I wasn't familiar with. Another rookie mistake was that I didn't lock my car doors. Some guy just walked up to the car, opened the door and started giving me the usual abuse about me being scum. He started punching me really hard in the face and trying to take the camera off me. As he was attacking me, I wrapped the strap of the camera around the steering wheel of the car and he was really pulling it and pulling me and violently and viciously punching me. That was a mistake, I should have just handed him the camera and let him go on with it. But I was adamant that he wasn't getting my camera.

The camera strap ripped with the force of it. Those straps are made to withstand anything, but he was really strong, and it just gave way. I started to panic then. He threw the camera at the windscreen of the car. The windscreen didn't even crack, but the camera broke when it fell on the ground. I saw it smash, and I thought, that's it, the camera is gone. I'm out of here. So, I drove away at high speed. But I didn't realise that the funeral cortege was still moving and was blocking my only way out of the cul-de-sac. The guy was chasing after me, still shouting and throwing bits of the camera at the car. So, I had driven at speed into a crowd of people, and I'm remembering the British Army corporals who were killed at the IRA funeral in west Belfast all those years ago. I thought I was going to be lynched and killed, genuinely. But thankfully the crowd parted like the Red Sea, and I got out of there.

That was one of the most terrifying experiences of my life. I was absolutely traumatised by that incident, this savage man beating me like that; feeling trapped and totally vulnerable. That was the one time I thought I was going to be killed. I couldn't sleep for ages after that. Being beaten up in my car was the lowest point of my career. I felt the most helpless and useless I had ever done. I felt stupid for putting myself in that position. But I learned lessons from it. I never go to anything like that on my own anymore. I always have someone with me, driving as I'm taking pictures. You learn as you go. But Dublin is a much more dangerous place than Belfast ever was. The criminals and gangsters have no code of ethics that paramilitaries might have had with the media. They will shoot you and kill you if you get in their way. That was a big lesson for me in how vicious things can quickly become. That was in broad daylight in the middle of a housing estate.

People might think why do you keep doing the job after all these things that have happened? But it's my career, it's something that I'm good at and it's something that I enjoy greatly. A lot of jobs have got a certain level of risk. Someone working on a building site could be killed by a JCB reversing over them. You do have to have a level of training and personal responsibility.

It is very difficult when you come home to switch off, particularly after covering really tough stories. I think that the one thing that helps me deal with the daily diet of misery is my son, Oisin. Simply having a chat with him and hearing the innocence of his conversations knocks me back into check and cheers me right up. He still doesn't have a clue about all this or about the Troubles. So that is what helps me shrug off a hard day's work, to hear a silly question from a five-year-old. If I've had a hard day, I make a beeline for Oisin and he helps me feel better, makes my day better. Kids have a habit of grounding you in the moment, they make you feel human and not caught up in whatever the big drama was that day.

I think resilience for me comes with each knock back. I think to myself, it didn't kill me. I'm not dead. I'm still here. The next one won't affect me as badly. I know how to deal with that particular situation now.

Every day in this job is a lesson.

Hope wins, even in the darkest of times

David Blevins

DAVID BLEVINS has more than 30 years experience as a reporter in Northern Ireland, and has been a Sky News Ireland Correspondent for two decades – interviewed by Leona O'Neill

"We broke the news and the news broke us."

I have been a journalist for over 30 years in Northern Ireland and as such covered all of the biggest news stories to come out of this place from Troubles to peace. But the stories that have stayed with me, that have haunted me are those where sheer evil and lack of humanity were glaring. We broke the news and at times the news broke us.

When I was growing up, I actually always wanted to be a teacher and my twin brother wanted to be a journalist. It's really bizarre that I ended up a journalist and he became a teacher. Between GCSEs and lower sixth year I got some work experience at a pirate radio station in Omeath in County Louth called Z103FM and that is really how I ended up falling in love with journalism and broadcasting. I loved the adrenaline and the immediacy around news.

I had very little experience of the Troubles because I grew up in the countryside just outside Portadown in a very non-sectarian home. My parents were not into the July celebrations, we didn't go to parades or bonfires. They had friends from both sides of the community. I was brought up in a Protestant family but we were always very cross-community. One of my brothers married a Catholic girl.

I did go to school in Portadown and a lot of my friends would have talked about bonfires and marches. I vividly remember in my school days all of the unrest around The Tunnel area of Portadown when the Orange Order march was first rerouted in the mid 80s. Ironically it was rerouted up past Drumcree, which subsequently became an even greater problem in later years.

My first journalism job was with the *Banbridge Chronicle*. Often when someone starts off in journalism in most normal situations, they get to do all the soft stories or are sent to cover the local petty sessions in court or council. But I think because in those days Northern Ireland was so full on, it was just relentlessly Troubles-related news and even the youngest and newest reporter in the newspaper office was sent out to shootings and bombings.

On my very first day as a reporter on Downtown Radio and Cool FM in October 1993, the Shankill bomb exploded.

Previous to that day I had been working as a newscaster in the studio. I had got bored after reading the news for two and a half years and had wanted to get back out into the thick of it again.

On my first shift back out as a reporter for them I had been sent to do a really routine story. A former Lord Mayor of Belfast had died and I was covering his funeral. I was standing in Roselawn Cemetery when I heard the bomb explode on the Shankill Road. I went straight there and it was absolute pandemonium. In fact, pandemonium would be an understatement in terms of what I was met with. There were police officers and local men trying to claw through the rubble to people who were trapped. The police were trying to establish a cordon and there were emergency services arriving. The media were beginning to arrive.

I remember it was around 10 minutes to the hour and I phoned the newsroom at Downtown from the street. They said to me that I wouldn't have time to write a report. They said that they were going to call me back in two minutes and were going to record an eyewitness account of what was happening to put out on the hour.

I remember vividly coming off the call and freezing with the sheer magnitude of what I was witnessing before my eyes. I became almost paralysed by what was happening around me. It was total chaos. I remember the BBC's Stephen Walker, a friend and colleague of mine, coming up to me. I confessed to him that I was about to do an eyewitness report and I really didn't know what to say. In that moment I thought to myself I can't do this; I have lost the ability to do this.

I remember Stephen's words to this day. He just said, "Say what you see" and that is what I did. The phone rang and I just said what I could see around me. I remember midway through that recording the body of a young female was carried past me by the emergency services as I stood on the street corner. There was a weird realisation that I didn't have time to stop and process what I had just seen or what was happening. I literally just had to keep talking. And for quite a long time after that I thought about that very moment in time. Every time I closed my eyes, I remembered that moment. I remembered that individual. It was horrific. I had nightmares about that day for a long time.

One thing about my career has been the relentless nature of what we do. I think the morning after the Shankill bombing there were two people shot in Belfast. A week after the bombing there was the Rising Sun pub shootings in Greysteel, County Derry. Back in those days you went so quickly from one tragedy to the next tragedy. It was like bombing and shooting, the aftermath of that, funeral and then the tit-for-tat and whatever would come next. It was just so relentless that you never really had time to process it until much later on. I feel that sometimes it's only now that I'm processing some of it.

Back in those days it was a relentless diet of daily bombings, shootings, funerals and then a period of time when we had the civil unrest whether that was around marching disputes or flags. I was working on rolling news where it was just constantly "fill, fill, fill" and they wanted to know what was happening in every single moment.

When the Omagh bomb happened in August 1998, I was on air within an hour and a half from the Belfast studio. My colleague Gary Honeyford went to Omagh with his crew and I went there 24 hours later. That night in Belfast was my longest ever continuous broadcast. I went on air at 5pm and came off at midnight and I was constantly talking to the presenter in London as they were rolling footage that Gary and his crew were feeding in from the scene. Those were the days we still used fax machines. I remember the ambulance service issued a fax and every hour the death toll rose. My job was to sit in that studio at the top of the hour and say that the ambulance service for Northern Ireland has just confirmed that the death toll has now reached nine, 11, 16, 17 and so on. It was difficult.

Mercifully I wasn't on the ground for the first 24 hours but I then spent the next week there talking to people who had been bereaved.

A week later I was driving to Omagh for the memorial service that had tens of thousands of people in attendance and where Juliet Turner sang the song Broken Things so beautifully. I will never hear that song without being transported straight back to that Omagh street. I think the words were so apt – "You can have my heart, if you don't mind broken things". I think we all realised the extent to which we were all broken that day.

That morning driving to Omagh, I think I had started to process it all. I suppose I was thinking through the fact I was going to be live on air for a long time at the memorial that day and what I might talk about. I thought about the stories that I had heard from the bereaved that whole previous week. I think it all began to build up and I guess it had to be released somehow. I remember beginning to cry. I had to stop the car and I cried my eyes out by the side of the road just outside Omagh. It was like it all just came to the surface at once. And I have never forgotten that moment.

During those years, our children were born and there was so much going on in my personal life at the same time. Our daughter was born six weeks before the Good Friday Agreement. Our eldest son was born 18 months later. So, we had a tiny baby in the house at the time of the Omagh bomb and something like that changes your life. I have no idea how I managed to work so relentlessly, somehow process all of what was happening and still be a husband and father to a newborn baby.

I think as journalists we all just kept going and often, we didn't process it. And I think that has been part of our problem for many of us in journalism. We had to just file the next report, do the next live broadcast, had to find another family who wanted to tell their story. I think we often didn't process what it was doing to us and then carry it with us for a long time.

In many ways talking now about it has been the most I have discussed any of this, ever. I have never discussed it with a therapist or a counsellor or a GP. I have probably only touched on it, even with my own family, only if they have asked. It was not really talked about back then, how stories can affect you. I think it's fair to say that a lot of news organisations these days are inundating their staff with notices telling them that if they are affected by stories that they can talk to occupation health or a mental health team. It's a bit like the message at the end of difficult programmes on the TV. But when we were covering wall-to-wall violent murders back in those days there was none of that. Nobody ever said, "How are you doing?"

I covered the marching disputes and related unrest at Drumcree, on the Lower Ormeau and in Ardoyne, flashpoints at Orange parades in Belfast. I've always said that you can cope much better with petrol bombs, because you can see them coming. But when you start to hear gunfire or they start throwing blast bombs, it's a completely different ballgame. You can't see them coming and you feel much more vulnerable.

I was in Ardoyne one night immediately after political parties were talking in England to deal with decommissioning. Some of us had been there for a week covering that and we had flown back to Belfast for the Orange Order parade in Ardoyne. It was shocking. The rioting was intense. Some 104 police officers fell in the space of an hour. That is how intense the violence was. I think about nights like that all the time. In those days we were not issued with protective gear. The international media were always in flak jackets and helmets whenever they were in the Middle East or in different parts of the world that were dangerous. But bizarrely it was not a standard issue in Northern Ireland. It was not how the media behaved until more recent years. So, in many ways it is miraculous that we didn't see more journalists killed. They just developed a knack of knowing how to take hard cover themselves and go where they could try to avoid getting hurt.

I was on the Garvaghy Road in Portadown in July 1997 when an RUC team was sent in at 3am to clear the road of protestors to push the Drumcree Orange Order parade through. I was there the moment it happened. There was a place there on that road and I remember another place on the Ormeau Road during violence there that acted as a no man's land. Very often the media found ourselves there. I remember on several occasions in the 1990s lying flat on the ground as petrol bombs were coming from one direction and plastic bullets were being fired from the other.

I don't ever recall lying on the ground trying to avoid a missile or a baton round being fired and thinking "I could die here". It is always in retrospect that the thought comes to your mind.

With the relentless nature of those periods of unrest, you lived in constant fear. But the antidote to the fear was the adrenaline of getting the best picture, the best audio, being able to tell the story properly. One dealt with the other. The adrenaline kicked in and you didn't get a chance to think about it all until much later.

I worked during the Drumcree crisis through the night for two years in a row and I got to see the worst of the violence because it was always at night that the shots were fired at the police or the rioting kicked off.

I think so often when I look back on those days that I definitely had a guardian angel looking over me.

I remember as a young reporter being sent to Crossmaglen in south Armagh one night. The IRA had shot a British Army helicopter down with an improvised mortar. Miraculously no one was killed. Travelling there it was pitch black dark, raining and miserable. On the way I got a puncture in the middle of nowhere. An old farmer stopped and helped me change the tyre. Then I got a second puncture. So, I'm there with a flat and no spare tyre, not knowing how I was going to get home.

There was an SDLP councillor who lived in Crossmaglen called John Fee and he was unusually vocal in condemning the IRA. He was a real gentleman. That night I interviewed him for my radio piece and told him I had two punctures. He told me to take his car to get home and run it back up to him the next evening after work. My car was out of action so I was going to borrow it but another journalist, Barbara McCann, came to the rescue with some puncture foam, got me back on the road and I didn't need to.

The following night, because he had been so critical of the IRA for their attack on the army helicopter, John was stopped on the road into Crossmaglen by the IRA, dragged out of his car and viciously beaten. That man never recovered from that attack. He later died a very young man. But I often think that I came within a whisker of driving his car into Crossmaglen that night to return his car.

Another time I remember my cameraman Kieran Gaffney and I had gone to west Belfast because we had heard there was some trouble there related to Drumcree.

We came across rioting on the Andersonstown Road and tried to turn the car. Some people surrounded the car and told us we had 30 seconds to get our stuff out. I remember standing on the path at 2am with about £30,000 worth of technical equipment beside us and watching as they took our crew car, put it across the road, opened the boot and were about to throw a petrol bomb in there to create a flaming barricade. Then a man in the crowd recognised my cameraman, as he had grown up in Andersonstown. He said to the gathered boys, "Look this is a media vehicle, you're not doing yourselves any favours".

Against all the odds we got the crew car back, loaded it back up and off we drove.

Another night that comes to mind is the one where the photographer Niall Carson was shot. We were standing beside him on the Newtownards Road the night he went down beside us. I remember the shots being fired, there were two bursts of gunfire and he was injured in the first one. We all pulled back quite quickly. The following morning my cameraman got out of bed, put on his jeans – and those were the days before skinny jeans – and found there was a bullet hole in them. The bullet had gone right through the loose part of the fabric in front of his shin and hadn't even skinned him. But that is how close he came, centimetres.

On another night in Ardoyne, I was standing beside a blast bomb seconds before it went off, injuring the BBC's Chris Lindsay and another media worker, Simon Taylor. I remember standing on the street in Ardoyne and chatting to Simon for around five minutes. I said goodbye and walked over to my crew car. Just as I opened the door, I heard the thud of the blast bombs that injured Simon and Chris. Simon suffered horrific, life-changing injuries. Ten seconds earlier I was standing right beside Simon. Those incidents alone make me think often that I must have had a guardian angel.

It really is miraculous that we have not seen more journalists injured in Northern Ireland. I don't know how we have got away with it for so long, with just two – Marty O'Hagan and Lyra McKee – so sadly and tragically killed. It's a miracle that we didn't see more people killed and injured.

When I look back, I covered the Shankill bombing for the radio, the Omagh bombing for the television and some of those big incidents that people around the world would remember. But the stories that have definitely left the biggest impact on me and that still haunt me to this day are those brutal killings, particularly the shootings carried out by paramilitaries in the 'Mid Ulster murder triangle'.

I would say the stories that haunt me the most were in the first five years of my career, because that was right at the tail end of the Troubles. It was the 1989-1994 period where it was really vicious just before the ceasefires. It was the murders of Eileen Duffy, aged 19, and Katrina Rennie, aged 17, in a mobile shop in Craigavon. It was Charles and Theresa Fox, an elderly couple murdered in Moy. It was Kathleen O'Hagan, a pregnant woman who was shot dead in Creggan, also in Tyrone. It was teenager Bernadette Martin, shot dead in bed next to her boyfriend in Aghalee or of Andrew Robb, aged 19, and David McIlwaine, aged 18, killed in Tandragee.

I couldn't figure out for a long time why those stories haunted me so much. I think it may have been about how indiscriminate they were. I don't believe any murder is justified but when you put on a uniform, I suppose you understand that there is a certain degree of risk. It was not justified in any sense, but there is something different about those murders than just two girls working in a mobile shop, or an elderly couple. I think what haunted me was the targeting of civilians for no other reason than their religion or because they were perceived to be something that they were not. It was just so brutal and callous. I think that the realisation that humans can do this to fellow humans was what haunted me.

Because they were in Armagh, Portadown, Lurgan, Craigavon and Dungannon and surrounding areas, I suppose you thought that they were just ordinary civilians who could be like you or your family. And because Northern Ireland is a village, they were like your neighbours. You really empathise with them because they are just ordinary people living in the countryside, in rural locations, which I've tended to live in all my life. And as such you realise how vulnerable these people were – elderly people or a pregnant woman. The heavily pregnant woman – who was the wife of a republican prisoner – was shot dead in front of her children as she bathed them. I suppose I was discovering for the first-time what hatred could do to a human being. The readiness to murder the most defenceless of civilians in the most brutal fashion imaginable – often for no other reason than their religion – represented an evil and a hatred that went way beyond my understanding of sectarianism.

If I'm honest I think the emotional barrier that was there for me was fear. I was security conscious after some of those incidents. Fear became the norm. I didn't report each murder and return to the safety of my home. I reported them and returned to the very town where those responsible lived and walked and socialised among us. Fear became a way of life. What if angry locals at the scene of this murder discover I'm from Portadown? What if the killers back in Portadown don't like how I've reported this?

These murders were largely carried out by the Mid Ulster unit of the Ulster Volunteer Force, run by Billy Wright, widely known as 'King Rat'. I had the fear on the ground while doing the story and then I had the fear when I got home that the UVF are not going to like how I reported the story. And the next door that is going to be kicked in is mine. The bullets are going to come through my window and target me and my family. I kind of felt the fear from both sides. There was a fear of my own personal background and also the fear of the loyalists in the town where I live not liking my reporting, and I was geographically close to them. And if they are going to be that blasé about who they target and how brutal they are, what's to stop them targeting me?

To the best of my knowledge, I only met Billy Wright once – on the night the UVF disbanded his unit for breaching the cease-fire and ordered him to leave town within 72 hours. He gave me his only television interview, saying: "I'm not afraid to die." Every time a car pulled into the cul-de-sac, I wanted to lie on the floor in case bullets came through the window.

People regularly have said to me over the years that they don't know if I'm Catholic or Protestant and I always think that that is the greatest test of your impartiality.

Having grown up in a non-sectarian family, I learned what hatred of another can do to a person's moral compass and that a divided community can become almost immune to the depravity among it. We didn't just report the news. We lived it. It wasn't just Northern Ireland's story. It was our story. We broke the news and the news broke us.

I don't think we process what we see as journalists nearly enough. There are some stories we haven't processed at all; some we have processed a bit. I survive by absolutely holding to the belief that there will always be more good people than bad. There is always more good than evil. I hold fast to that. And I think I've seen that, even though I've seen the most awful, awful horrors. I have also come across so many extraordinary people.

Gordon Wilson, whose daughter Marie was one of 11 people killed in the IRA bombing of the Remembrance Day ceremony in Enniskillen in November 1987, said something the year before I entered journalism. He said: "I bear no ill-will, I bear no grudge."

I have come across countless Gordon Wilson type moments along the way: whether it's Michael Gallagher, who speaks so graciously and eloquently for the bereaved in Omagh; or Michael McGoldrick, who lost his son in a loyalist gun attack, saying that he and his wife forgave his killers and prayed for them every night. I've come across people like that time and time again and it makes me think, evil does not win in the end and there is still more good than bad.

These days I find myself looking for stories of hope and I love telling hopeful stories. There is just so much horror around us, and maybe because I have reported horror for so long, I love finding people who surprise us.

In Northern Ireland, particularly when you are reporting for an international audience, we hear only from the extremists, who shout the loudest and have the most extreme views. But I don't think they represent the majority of the population. I think the majority of people live somewhere in the middle. And I have tried to find the story in the middle. I seek out hope in the middle of adversity. Hope wins. I truly believe that. And I think that is how I've done any processing and how I live with it, because I believe ultimately that good will prevail.

The things I saw changed me as a reporter

Ivan Little

IVAN LITTLE has been a journalist for over 30 years in Northern Ireland, working with the *Belfast Telegraph*, Downtown Radio and UTV

> *"I was only able to look at the wall of death
> for a fleeting moment but even now I can still see
> the images in my mind's eye."*

It was like taking a wrong turn into hell as the apocalyptic sight of flattened houses and luxury hotels seared the eyes for what seemed like an eternity in tsunami-ravaged Phuket.

The devastation for 25 miles along the heavenly Thai coastline that had just days earlier been the playground of the rich and famous celebrating Christmas 2004, looked like a scene from a dystopian Hollywood movie. Nothing had been left standing.

But surveying that scorched earth landscape of nuclear holocaust proportions didn't challenge my emotions half as much as what lay ahead four miles inland.

I'd thought that reporting on 9/11 in New York a few years earlier and on the worst of Northern Ireland's Troubles like Omagh, Enniskillen, the Shankill bomb, Greysteel, the massacre at Graham's bookies, Loughinisland and countless other atrocities would steel me, prepare me for anything, anywhere.

But how wrong I was. For I discovered that I wasn't unshockable when our driver Seng pulled up at a richly colourful and ornately decorated Buddhist temple that had escaped the unrelenting wrath of the tsunami.

Outside there were what can only be described as mountains of unidentified, unclaimed bodies which hadn't yet made it into hastily-erected air-conditioned facilities under canvas or indoors. Some of the corpses were covered loosely in white sheets, others were wrapped in plastic and large containers of ice were scattered on top of them in a hopeless bid to preserve them from the uncompromising heat.

The assault on all of the senses was almost impossible to describe to anyone who didn't have to endure them.

But suffice to say that scientists had advised people who were near the bodies to inhale three sharp intakes of breath which they claimed would allow their noses to "eventually adjust to the smells".

Also, at that first temple what had been a surround-sound of silence was suddenly shattered by the noise of the hammering of men returning to their tasks of making rudimentary coffins which were stacked high to await the bodies that would eventually fill them.

The coffin-makers were prisoners freed from jails to undertake their grim but all-too-necessary jobs.

The post-tsunami scenes I saw in Thailand were undoubtedly replicated in hundreds of makeshift mortuaries around southeast Asia where the death toll from the merciless tsunami was to reach a mind-numbing 230,000.

At another temple at Khao Lak, Thai workers who were clad head to toe in protective clothing pushed handcarts loaded with body-bags as distraught relatives followed them for forensic teams from around the world to try to positively identify their loved ones.

Outside the temple, clusters of bewildered souls who were desperately looking for missing family members scanned noticeboards that the authorities had covered with stomach-wrenching montages of photographs of bodies. Many of the grotesquely bloated faces appeared beyond recognition especially the ones of tiny babies and toddlers. I was only able to look at the wall of death for a fleeting moment but even now I can still see the images in my mind's eye. At one point along a major highway through Phuket my UTV cameraman Albert Kirk and I stopped at what had already become a striking tsunami landmark, which millions of global television viewers had seen on news bulletins.

It was a Thai navy patrol boat that had been swept contemptuously by the killer waves several miles inland where it still stands today as a memorial to the victims and to the awesome power of the tsunami.

Not far away the emergency services were searching a lagoon for cars and their passengers who had been hurled to their doom from the highway. It was distressing to film relatives who watched in total and abject silence, hoping for a miracle they knew wasn't going to come.

I'd gone to Thailand after the Boxing Day catastrophe that I'd seen unfold in horrifying amateur video footage which holidaymakers had captured from high ground as the tsunami sent waves crashing ashore wrecking everything in their path and engulfing people who'd attempted to sprint for their lives or had clung to anything they could in forlorn efforts to survive.

Albert and I had travelled to Phuket with the family of Cookstown man Connor Keightley, who'd gone missing on

Phi Phi Island from where he'd sent Christmas greetings to his family. His sisters Darina and Michelle, his uncle Damian Coyle and cousin Gavin O'Neill invited us to record their search for 30-year-old Connor, whom they hoped might have been languishing in a remote hospital suffering from amnesia.

At one hospital the sisters' spirits soared as they spotted a photograph among the pictures of injured survivors and we all agreed that the man looked uncannily like Connor. Sadly, the hospital staff later told us that the man was, in fact, Swedish.

Ireland's Department of Foreign Affairs provided magnificent back-up and the Ambassador, Dan Mulhall, was a tower of strength for the family, even hiring a speedboat to take them, and us, from the town of Krabi to Phi Phi.

In normal times the journey in blisteringly glorious sunshine across the hypnotically blue Andaman Sea would have been a once-in-a-lifetime experience to savour but those were anything but normal times. And any shreds of optimism that Connor might somehow have survived the tsunami disintegrated almost instantly as we inched into dock at the hippy island of dreams which was now the stuff of nightmares.

Sunken boats littered the bay and on shore five-star hotels, trendy shops, cosmopolitan cafes, beach bars and backpacker hostels including one where Connor had probably been staying, had been ripped apart. We picked our way through the detritus and the sisters showed people pictures of Connor in the hope that they might ring a bell but many of them were too busy fleeing Phi Phi to take time to look at the photographs.

Out of the blue the sisters saw somewhere they recognised, the stretch of beach in the photo that Connor had sent to Tyrone with him sitting beside his Christmas message scrawled in the sand. Darina and Michelle stood in a poignant, prayerful contemplation on the beach clinging to each other for support before gathering up shells to give to loved ones back home as cherished mementoes of the brother they, by that time, realised couldn't still be alive.

After three horrendous hours on Phi Phi Island the search was now for Connor's body and the Irish Foreign Minister Dermot Ahern met the Keightleys to assure them that a team of visiting Garda forensic experts would do everything they could for them. In many ways, it was like looking for a needle in a horrible haystack.

The first priority was to liaise with mortuaries to establish if a body matching Connor's description had been found. Forensic scientists from all around the world were staying, as Albert and I were, in Thailand's biggest hotel, the Hilton Arcadia at Karon beach which hadn't been damaged by the tsunami. The hotel's opulence was stunning but we had neither the time nor the heart to indulge ourselves in its luxury and the nightly entertainment seemed incongruous. Listening to a girl band singing Abba's greatest hits just a few miles from where thousands of bodies lay unidentified, felt totally wrong.

On our one night off Albert and I had a meal and a couple of drinks in the quiet downtown area of Karon where we played Connect Four with Thai girls who bemoaned the lack of male tourists that normally paid for connections of a very different kind. Shortly afterwards things took a tragic but perhaps inevitable twist as the Keightleys were summoned to the Pearl Hotel in the centre of Phuket. Our driver Seng took the family and us to the drab hotel where a grim-faced Dan Mulhall was waiting.

And as the Keightleys went to meet him in a side room, I asked Albert to stop filming for the first time in the entire trip. The sound of the sisters' anguished cries confirmed that they had just been given the worst possible news, that Connor's body had been located.

The Irish officials revealed that body number 467 in a mortuary in Krabi had been identified as Connor from his dental records, a distinctive tattoo on his back and a Storm watch on his wrist. The Keightleys were offered their own transport back to the Hilton so that they could come to terms with the sad disclosure on their own.

But Darina and Michelle said they wanted to travel back with me and Albert in our minibus. They said we'd been with them from the start of their journey and they wanted us to be with them at the finish. They added they'd come to Thailand as a family of four but were returning to Ireland as a family of six.

Albert and I were both overwhelmed. It was indeed like losing one of our own. Unusually we'd crossed the line from chroniclers of a news story to being at the heart of it.

For Darina and Michelle, the discovery of Connor's body meant that they could grieve but there was also a sense of relief that they could bring their brother home to their parents.

That night after Albert and I had edited our news package and I had done a live two-way interview with UTV in Belfast, we joined the Keightleys to wake Connor with a send-off that lasted until breakfast-time.

After two hours sleep, I sat on the beach for the first time at Karon and amid the serenity and the beauty I tried to imagine what it had been like just a short time earlier to see the towering waves hurtling in with all their frightening fury.

The journey home via Bangkok and Munich passed in a blur and at home sleep proved elusive over the next few days as the tragedy replayed in my head.

Albert and I quickly set about making a half-hour documentary about the tsunami and we attended Connor's funeral in Cookstown, as mourners not as journalists.

Monsignor Raymond Murray read a message from the Keightleys thanking Albert and me for our support and sensitivity. They were words I'd never heard before at a funeral.

Back in Belfast I invited my neighbours and their children into my home to watch footage that Albert had taken of me handing over money to a charity trying to help victims of the tsunami. The cash had been collected by the kids at a number of fund-raising events around the neighbourhood.

And I was later to meet children orphaned by the tsunami. Seven of them travelled to Northern Ireland in 2015 to thank people here for funding their education.

The manager of the popular Harbour Bar in Portrush, Willie Gregg was the driving force behind the charity Willie's Orphan Fund, which raised tens of thousands of pounds for the Baan Than Namchai home in Khao Lak.

Willie went back and forward to Thailand with aid after the disaster and brought seven of the children here; at one point they paid a touching tribute to the late Radio Ulster presenter Gerry Anderson who was a passionate supporter of the orphans.

The youngsters spent 45 minutes with Gerry's widow Christine and daughter Kirsty at his final resting place in the City Cemetery in Derry/Londonderry.

I reported on the trip for the *Belfast Telegraph* and wrote how the children followed a simple but uplifting Thai tradition of scattering petals over Gerry's grave before singing the song that had become the unofficial anthem of the orphanage, 'Stay the Way You Are' written by Coleraine man Uel Walls.

As for the Keightleys, I stayed in touch with them and wrote a number of stories about them on anniversaries of Connor's death which they marked with a series of tributes and the setting up of an award at Belfast College of Art where he'd been a prize-winning student.

However, the most difficult follow-up article that I had to write was about his mother Teresa who rang me regularly for a chat. From those conversations it was clear that Teresa had never got over Connor's death and the impact that it had had on her family.

In December 2018 Teresa went missing in Cookstown and several days later the Community Rescue Service found the body of one of the last victims of the tsunami, 14 years after the southeast Asian horror.

Just a few years before the tsunami, I reported on what I was certain – wrongly as it transpired – would be the biggest world disaster that I would ever cover.

When you work for a small regional station like Ulster Television you do not expect to find yourself in all parts of the world to cover stories like 9/11 in New York.

I'd been in a dry cleaner's shop collecting a suit when I heard a news flash on a radio about aircraft flying into one of the Twin Towers in Manhattan. Like thousands of other people, I assumed it was an accident. But that thought vanished after I saw live pictures on my television of a second plane smashing into the World Trade Centre (WTC), little thinking that shortly afterwards I would be standing on the very same streets.

Ulster Television managed to get me, my cameraman Brian McVeigh and researcher Mary Curry booked on the first Aer Lingus flight out of Ireland to New York. As we queued at Belfast International Airport ground staff were offering compensation to passengers who would give up their seats to Americans trying to get home to be with their families. We had to say no and when we reached Shannon Airport for a stop-over the atmosphere was even more surreal.

Hundreds of American soldiers, who were being flown into bases in Europe and further afield readying themselves for God knows what, wandered around the terminal many of them in a daze. One serviceman in front of me in a shop bought a little sew-on badge with a shamrock and the word Ireland emblazoned on it.

"It might just be my last souvenir of anywhere," he told the assistant.

The flight to New York from Shannon was unnerving. No-one had the slightest idea of what we were flying into, and Aer Lingus attendants said they had volunteered for the flight after the company insisted they wouldn't force any employees to man it. On touch down in New York I joined in a Benidorm-style round of applause from the relieved passengers for the crew. The taxi ride into Manhattan into NYC was terrifying as smoke still billowed from the famous skyline which pitifully had two enormous gaps where the Twin Towers should have stood.

I cajoled Brian and Mary to join me for a 5.30am start, only hours after we'd checked into the iconic Fitzpatrick's Hotel on Lexington Avenue. The nearest we could get to Ground Zero in the morning was Canal Street, just a few blocks away from the carnage and even there the stench of smoke and death was choking, forcing many people to don masks.

Despite the early hour the area was full of bleary-eyed rescue teams walking to and from the epicentre of the disaster as massive trucks hauled huge girders away from the scene. Any concerns that the rescuers wouldn't want to talk to us were swiftly dispelled and an Irish American firefighter called Timothy O'Toole gave me my first interview, the gist of which still echoes around my head from time to time.

His face covered in dirt and wreathed in anguish, he told me: "My brothers are dying in there. It's horrible. I am hoping that people in there are going to be alright but as the days go on it's getting worse and worse. I am not the same person I was a few days ago. I have turned to God. I am praying to God every day."

Timothy from Engine 451 squad was clearly struggling to cope with what he had seen at Ground Zero but he declined to speak in detail about what it was like.

"I don't tell anyone," he said.

Another rescue worker Frank Segarra told me: "It's still smoking in there at the bottom and then suddenly a 30-foot flame will just jump up. For anybody to come out of there alive would be a miracle from God."

As the massive 24/7 operation went on at Ground Zero, office workers started returning on subways to work in buildings which were outside the sealed-off area. Talking to them was like a flashback to home as I discovered that the people of New York, just like countless folk back in Northern Ireland, had an unshakeable determination to show the terrorists that they wouldn't win.

However, all around New York people were carrying posters with photographs of loved ones who were missing, feared dead in the twin strikes at the Twin Towers.

They thrust the pictures in front of our camera and I gave up telling them their chances of anyone in Northern Ireland having information about their relatives were slim. That afternoon we went to St Patrick's Cathedral on Fifth Avenue to film outside a memorial service for 343 firefighters who were known, at that early stage, to have been lost as the North and South towers collapsed.

Thousands of New Yorkers cheered as the firefighters emerged solemnly from the Cathedral and again the missing persons' photographs were held up by relatives, including

Mickey Kirby whose fire-fighter son, Chris, and a friend Brian Monaghan hadn't come home after the attacks. I included shots of Mickey's poster in my report and astonishingly a family in Northern Ireland got in touch with UTV to say that Brian had close ties to Belfast which he had visited a short time earlier. It was eventually confirmed that Chris and Brian were both dead.

Soon afterwards one of the most sobering parts of the 9/11 story hit us as we visited a hospital which had been put on full alert after the planes crashed into the WTC.

A spokesman said the hospital hadn't been busy because the stark truth was that most people in the Twin Towers had either got out unharmed or had died. The injured list wasn't long.

I recorded a piece to camera at the hospital saying the authorities were expecting the death toll to top 6,000, and it struck me that more people had been killed inside a few minutes in New York than had died in all the years of the Troubles.

In the end it was confirmed that the actual number of people who had died was just under 3,000 and many bodies were never recovered because the victims were vaporised.

In the next days in New York we tracked down people from Northern Ireland who had been caught up in the nightmare of 9/11 like restaurant owners Eugene Devlin and Ronan Downs, who gave sanctuary in their eatery called Beckett's to people as they ran away from the storm of dust after the WTC collapsed a short distance away.

Conor Powell, a chef who was originally from Warrenpoint, told of the panic that gripped the survivors after rumours spread that five more planes were on their way to the city.

We later met Myles Donnelly from Enniskillen who had been in his office on the 78th floor of the South Tower when he saw the first plane smash into the North Tower.

Myles, a credit manager with Baseline Financial Services, told me that his experiences of growing up in Northern Ireland during the Troubles, including the Enniskillen bombing, probably saved his life because his first instinct was to get out of the South Tower even though some of his colleagues cautioned him to stay.

Myles, whose boss was among the people who perished, said he found a veritable war zone outside his building and he ran to find his wife who worked nearby.

Ten years after 9/11, Myles spoke to me during a break back home but he said that the trauma still haunted him and he didn't like to revisit that fateful day.

The most remarkable Northern Irishman I met in the Big Apple was a complete inspiration amid the gloom. Roger Smyth was a paramedic from the Antrim Road area of north Belfast and saw the grim events unfolding at the WTC from the roof of his apartment across the river in Brooklyn. Roger said he knew there and then that despite the risks he had to go to Manhattan to tend to the dead and dying and he also took a memorable photograph of firefighters raising the Stars and Stripes flag on top of the rubble, a copy of which hangs in my home.

Roger's reward for his courage was to be allowed to stay in the United States even though he didn't have the proper papers and the former Irish President Mary McAleese presented him with a bravery award in the Plaza Hotel in NYC. Quite incredibly, Roger's emergency services badge number was 9110 and three years later to the very day after the WTC attacks on 9/11 2004 Hurricane Ivan wrecked his new home on the Cayman Islands where he had been on a paramedic contract but again his first thoughts were for the survivors.

Back in New York, we uncovered another sad Northern Irish angle to 9/11 after a priest I had arranged to interview in the Bronx arrived late.

He apologised profusely and explained the reason for his delay was that he had to deal with the suicide of a parishioner who turned out to be from Northern Ireland.

As the days went on and we continued to report on Al Qaeda's murderous slaughter, it was still proving difficult to comprehend the scale of the tragedy that transformed New York into a city which was nothing like the one I'd known from previous visits. The always deafening and bustling metropolis was relatively silent after 9/11, with no horns blaring and with no motorists exchanging insults. One taxi driver even admitted he didn't know how to respond after other motorists waved him on into their lanes.

American flags appeared everywhere and people drove hundreds of miles to set up soup kitchens and to lay flowers at shrines in parks and on street corners. But the patriotism was matched by an almost palpable hunger for revenge.

Newspapers carried pictures of Osama bin Laden on their front pages alongside 'Wanted Dead or Alive' headlines. There was fear too. The sound of an overhead plane sparked alarm and the familiar places like the usually jam-packed Times Square were deserted at night and Broadway theatres were empty.

One show which was forced to close was Marie Jones' hit comedy *Stones in His Pockets*, which I'd championed from its debut in the Feile in Belfast to the West End of London.

My crew and I went to see the show as a little light relief but at the interval we made the mistake of going to a bar beside the theatre for a drink. On the television President George W Bush was giving an address to the nation in which he essentially declared war on the world of terrorism. Brian, Mary and I were scared rigid. All we wanted to do was get home as fast as possible before we were all ensnared in conflict. But even so I still dragged Brian and Mary backstage to meet the stars of *Stones*, Conleth Hill and Sean Campion, only to hear even more bad news.

Conleth, who's from Ballycastle in County Antrim, told me that his father, the mercurial BBC cameraman Patsy Hill whom I greatly admired, was perilously close to death at home. Not surprisingly, Conleth didn't feel up to doing an interview with me about the shutting down of the play. Sean, however, said the closure of *Stones* seemed almost inconsequential compared to what had happened at the Twin Towers.

As we left the theatre a woman approached me to ask if my partner, Siofra O'Reilly, was from Newry and if she was the daughter of a retired doctor from the town.

My confirmation brought an introduction to a member of her theatre-going group, Niall Feeley, who was to give me a chilling interview about 9/11. He was a construction worker who had darted from the basement of the WTC after hearing an explosion and in the process witnessed the sickening spectacle of dozens of people jumping to their deaths from the infernos at the Towers.

Getting back to Belfast from New York didn't get New York out of my mind. I had a documentary to make but for some reason the faces and names that I had seen in the missing posters wouldn't leave me. I had to find who they were and what became of them in an attempt to personalise 9/11.

In the next days and weeks I felt I came to know the likes of Victor Barbosa, a 23-year-old runner in the Windows on the World restaurant on top of the World Trade Centre. He was also a part-time rapper in a band called Silex. Others I tracked down on the internet included Craig Gibson, the Australian who loved Liverpool FC; Tonyell McDay, the pretty gospel singer who was just about to record an album; and Avnish Patel, the English-born Indian whose friends said he had a million dollar smile.

Like Victor Barbosa they were all confirmed as victims.

In the weeks and months after the plane attacks, it became clear that the backlash against terrorism in the States had also hardened America's attitude to the IRA and Sinn Fein.

The day that changed the world forever changed everything for terrorists all over the planet and some commentators said 9/11 pushed paramilitaries in Northern Ireland closer to peace.

From a personal perspective, reporting on two of the world's most gruesome tragedies in New York and Thailand – as well as covering the wars in Iraq and Afghanistan – undoubtedly changed me as a reporter. But I like to think that I have come through it all without suffering too much trauma. And though my experiences form part of after-dinner speeches that I give, I also include a lighter anecdote or two.

My favourite story was about the time I was waiting on a street in New York for an interviewee and a man who'd been drinking in a nearby pub came out and wondered if I was "the big fucker who used to read the news on UTV".

I said yes and he brought several of his friends from the bar to meet me after using the same colourful language to describe me. The men were all from Bellaghy and it proved to me that no matter where I go in the world I will forever be known to some people as the "big fucker who used to read the news on UTV".

The icing on the cake came when one of the Bellaghy boys was sent out again to ask me another question: "What's this your name is?"

The 'what ifs' haunt you forever

Peter Doherty

PETER DOHERTY has been a camera operator in Northern Ireland for more than 20 years – interviewed by Leona O'Neill

"Those bullets are really close, keep your fucking head down."

This job can affect you. I have woken myself up shouting some nights. I don't know what triggers it. There are some times I wake the entire house up warning people, shouting "look out" and "get back" and other things. When I wake up I can't remember what I was dreaming about, what was going through my head or what brought it on.

I remember one day out on a job in Belfast, during street disturbances, I could hear a noise like ripping and cracking above my head. I looked up and could see the leaves of the tree just ripping apart and the branches were cracking and falling off. I said to my colleague "are they shooting?" and he told me to wise up, they couldn't be. Then the cameraman in front of us jumped down from the barrier we were all standing on and ran, he said that a bullet just whizzed by his face. We all ducked, ran and took cover behind army jeeps.

There was trouble that day over an Orange Order march that had been stopped. There was a line of police about 300 yards up the road and a line of army about 100 yards from us. We had been in the Shankill earlier that morning filming and overheard someone say "we're going to put on some show today". Little did I know we would be in the middle of that particular show.

We stayed for another hour and I poked my head and the camera up just once to try to capture some audio. A photographer, I don't actually know who he was, grabbed me by the shoulders and pulled me down to the ground. He said he was in Sarajevo and said that if a bullet sounds as if it is in front of you, it hasn't reached you yet, and if it sounds like they are coming from behind you, they are going over your head. He told me: "Those bullets are really close, keep your fucking head down."

We got out of there shortly afterwards, cut it for the six o'clock news and I drove home. I think it was only when I was on the road I started to think about what had happened. Our daughters were still little and they ran and gave me hugs when I came in the door. It's only when I got back to normality, back home among my family, that it started to sink in. I remember sitting on my sofa with the girls playing on the floor thinking, how close was that? I thought, genuinely, I might not have come home.

The last time I was in Ardoyne there was a panic about a gunman on top of the shop roof. I had positioned myself on top of a wall to get the best footage. I was thinking, if there is a gunman I'm going to get a great shot, but I'm also in the firing line. The police were on top of the shops, edging forward with their automatic weapons poised and I was there filming it all. It turned out two young men had got onto the roof and had a crowbar. The crew in the helicopter thought it was a gun. When you think about these things afterwards, you think, what the Hell was I doing there, standing filming when there was a chance a gunman was right in front of me?

It's weird after all these years, all those experiences, kind of blend into one another. All the Ardoynes, the Drumcree disputes, the riots and street disturbances in north and east Belfast; trouble, wherever it is. I remember being somewhere, it might have been north Belfast and a policeman said "take hard cover" and myself and another cameraman got down behind the police vehicle. I looked around at all these young reporters, shooting footage on their mobile phones still standing in the street. They were looking at us and saying "what are you doing?" and we had to explain to them that they needed to get behind something hard right now because the army were going to do a controlled explosion.

There was another time in Ardoyne there was a full-scale riot happening in the street. I had to run my tape down to the satellite van and when I came back up, the street where the riot was just minutes before was deserted. I thought, where is everyone? But then I looked down the street and saw that it would make a really great shot: a big empty street with rubble everywhere, smoke coming from a barricade, completely deserted. So I set up my tripod in the middle of the road and started filming. I could hear this insistent "Peter" being shouted from somewhere. But I was too focused on what I was trying to do. I shouted "hold on a second until I get my shot". Then it was more panicked.

"Peter! Peter! Move! They are shooting down the road!" I lifted the tripod and ran. They had started shooting, everyone had run, I came around the corner and just set up my tripod in an eerily quiet street after everyone had taken cover.

Ever since I was a kid I always wanted to be a camera operative, although I had imagined myself doing music videos or TV programmes. When I got into my late teens someone said I'd make a good news cameraman because I was tall and had big shoulders. And there was always work in news. I started off in Channel 9 in Derry and then moved onto other news outlets. I remember one of the first stories that I did with a large news broadcaster that I knew was powerful and would make a difference. There was an elderly woman scammed out of quite a lot of money. It was a powerful interview. She was upset and she had said that it was the money she was going to use for her funeral. It was a really hard-hitting interview. And we got back to the studio and we were cutting it and we knew we had something powerful and emotive that would make a change and it felt good to give her a voice.

The story that stands out in my head was the thwarted attack on Parliament Buildings at Stormont in 2006 by loyalist killer Michael Stone, who had been released from prison along with other paramilitaries following the Good Friday Agreement. I was there that day and filmed it all. We were all standing in the Great Hall in Stormont. There was BBC, UTV, ITN, TG4, Sky and me. These were the days before there were televisions in the Great Hall and I remember turning to someone and saying that we were going to be the last to know what was happening.

Then I heard shouting and swearing coming from outside the front door. I immediately thought it was protestors. I was standing behind my camera and I was trying to click the audio cable out of the back of it and it seemed to take me forever, but was probably about five seconds. I switched on my camera, put it on my shoulder and spun around just as the two security personnel had Michael Stone stuck in the door. They were holding his hand and one of them had a handgun in her other hand. I ran towards them and stood at the top of the step. I zoomed into the gun and zoomed out wide. I was thinking, what the Hell is going on here? but I just keep filming anyway.

Exactly where I was standing at the top of the steps Stone had thrown a rucksack with two coffee jar bombs in it. They were fizzing. I didn't know that at the time, I didn't even see the bag. I was just concentrating on filming what was happening, getting the best shots, and literally nothing else.

The security teams came out of the side doors and one of them shoved me in the chest in the rush to get everyone out. They were shouting "Move! Move! Move! Everyone out!" and they pushed us down towards the east door to get out. I was recording the whole time because I was waiting for something to explode and wanted to capture it on audio.

It was just another instance where I could have been injured. Stone could have come in and fired off a few shots while we had our backs to him. The gun was a replica, but you do think. And also, the bag with the explosives could have gone off right beside me. It was a replica weapon, but the coffee jar bombs were real. When you see someone standing with a gun, you don't automatically think, that's a replica, but still we stood there and filmed.

I remember going out of Stormont, getting my footage away and everyone saying "that's brilliant, great footage, well done". Then the adrenaline goes away and you're left sitting there thinking, Jesus, I could have been killed just then. It was only then that someone told me about the bag with the bombs in it at my feet. You think and think about it. It's the 'what if?' stuff. When the adrenaline and the bravado are there all you are thinking about is getting the best shot, you have no thought of your own safety. It's weird and it's dangerous.

Out in the field I have been hit on the head with stones and golf balls. Double A batteries used to be a thing they would throw. I think it was because the police would search people going towards a protest and they would obviously confiscate the golf balls, but they can't stop them having batteries, because they would say they were for their Walkman or whatever. So we got pelted with them for a long time. I have been hit in the head a few times with golf balls and even when the adrenaline is flying it's still sore, but you keep going. It's not until afterwards when you touch the top of your head or someone says there is a massive lump or a bruise that you realise it was a really hard thump you got.

We are provided with a lot of protective gear but we don't like to use it. It's heavy, it slows you down and you are more of a target with an army helmet on; a flak jacket makes you look like a police officer.

I was in Belfast City Hall the night that the flag protestors tried to break in and the trouble erupted. The City Council had voted to restrict the number of days the Union Flag could be flown over City Hall, and there was a ferocious backlash from loyalists. We were all in there and the vote to take down the flag went through. We all said that we needed to get out of there and get a few vox pops outside to get a sense of what people were feeling about it.

We went downstairs and the security told us that we couldn't get out that there was a crowd there. Then the security team came in through the back gates and one of the guys had a cut on his head and was bleeding badly. They locked the doors and all of a sudden the stained glass windows started smashing as stones came in. A crowd started to break in the back doors and we're standing there filming and the glass from the windows are coming in on top of us. There was a woman shouting "no surrender" in through the smashed window. And we're all standing there basically trapped inside and someone shouts to open the front doors as the police are coming in with dogs in case the protestors actually got into the building. So as the police and dogs came in, I ran out past them to capture what was happening outside.

I captured some of the worst trouble there that night as the rioting spilled out onto the streets. As I was filming the photographer Peter Morrison walked up past me, his head bloody, he was badly hurt. He had got hit by a police truncheon on the head. He was being walked up the street by a police medic who dressed his wounds and bandaged him up. We went up to the office and cut the footage as quickly as we could, knowing that everyone was stuck in City Hall and we would get the first pictures out.

You're always looking towards a deadline and it's only in the aftermath you think that what happened during the day was rough, that you could have been hurt. I sometimes think that if you don't get hurt, you just keep going. I have known people who have been seriously hurt and they have said, "I can't do this anymore". I understand that and I don't blame them at all. Getting hurt is always in the back of your mind in this job. I don't know if it's a case of thinking it will never happen to me but look at Lyra McKee, just standing there. It could very easily happen to any of us.

I still think this job is the best in the world. No two days are the same. There is good and bad in not knowing where you are going to end up, who you are going to meet. I would do a variety of coverage – from sport to entertainment to news – so for every riot I was in, I also did something brilliant. I've met Bruce Springsteen, Nick Kershaw, Alex Ferguson and so many others. You get to see behind the scenes at things. I've been in the changing room of Croke Park at the Ulster and All-Ireland finals. I'm not a big of Gaelic sports but I know so many people would give their right arm to do that.

This job can see you go anywhere and cover anything. Yes I've been at riots, been shot at, almost blown up a couple of times but I also filmed an exorcism. Not many people can say they did that. It was at a house in Mid Ulster, in a brand-new estate, a lovely cul-de-sac. The owners told us that when we were bringing in our equipment to bring them in in bags so as not to alert the neighbours. It was a very quiet area.

The family were anonymous, filmed in shadow. They told us about what was happening. They would leave and come home and all the pictures would be turned towards the wall. Things would start moving while they were sitting there, a coffee table started spinning, there were symbols and markings scratched on the door and walls. The family wouldn't stay in the house at night. There was a retired Church of Ireland minister there with us. He put on the garb, got out the cross and chalices and did his service. I was filming and there were doors upstairs banging loudly, there were loud crashes from above us. It was an experience, that's for sure, and I absolutely loved it.

I think in some ways we get addicted to the adrenaline buzz of a story in a way. Sometimes I hear sirens and I think "they are playing my tune" and off I go. You put pressure on yourself to be the first there, to get the best shots and to have your pictures out first. That also drives you.

The one story that still stays with me is the murder of Michaela McAreavey in Mauritius. I would have known Michaela from covering the GAA. She would have been at events helping out on media and press nights. I know when someone dies people say they were a great person, but Michaela really was so nice, so friendly and so down to earth. She would have gone around us making sure we had everything we needed and chatted to everyone. We all got to know her. She just seemed to have a really nice way about her and would have talked to you like she knew you all your life. So then to hear that she was murdered on her honeymoon at a luxury resort, it was horrendous. We went over and had to cover the murder trial and how it all ended and it was very difficult.

I always find funerals hard to cover. There is a human interest in those, but you do feel like you are intruding in people's grief. But everyone watches on the news and you are trying your damnedest to be respectful.

Sometimes going to tragedies and accidents can be difficult. People's emotions are raised. I remember covering a tragic farming accident once and one of the neighbours of the deceased tried to run me over in his tractor. We were around 500 yards away from the house where the tragedy happened. Another man came up and started shouting at us, asking what we were doing. We told him we were there to cover the accident. I told him we were just trying to do our job and we will keep a respectful distance. He got into his tractor and drove up the road, turned around and drove back down towards us again. As he neared us he swerved into us in his tractor and we all ended up in a ditch, cameras and all, to avoid an eight-foot tyre. One of our crew went up to him later that day and said that we were thinking of phoning the police, that he almost hit us. He apologised and said that the man who died was his friend. He could have killed us.

In this job you get to see the worst side of humanity every day. That can impact on you. I do remember one time being at a riot, looking around me at what was happening, the violence and the hate. I remember a feeling come over me, I just thought "I don't know if I can do this anymore". I had just witnessed a policeman being really badly injured and I remember thinking how can someone do that to another human being? The people doing this don't know and they don't care who they hurt. I remember lifting the camera off my shoulder and just looking around, really thinking I didn't want to do it anymore. I was just fed up with all the hate. I walked away for five or ten minutes, gathered myself and I went back at it again, put my camera back on my shoulder and started filming. I just kept going.

The nature of news is that you might get a story the next day that will lift your spirits and remind you why you do this job in the first place. For every riot there was Daniel O'Donnell's wedding in Kincasslagh, there was Daisy the cow in south Down. The stories you think "why am I doing this?" and then it ends up being the best fun and you laugh the whole way back to the office, you laugh constantly cutting it and it goes down well with viewers. You sometimes get a better and longer buzz off a nice, uplifting, lighter story. It makes you think you did something good.

I've been all over the world and I think I'm so lucky in what I do. I've been in East Timor, Kuala Lumpur, Dubai, Bahrain. I got to the World Cup in Germany. There are plenty of stories you cover where you think people are amazing. They do things above and beyond what is needed.

There are also days when you wonder what people are thinking. I remember working outside City Hall a few weeks back and a man came over and spat on me. I asked him if he was alright and he just walked away. I think the social media conspiracy theories on the media are crazy. The last few months I've been told I'm paid by Bill Gates, that I was a disgrace and that no one can believe anything we say. There seems to be an awful lot of hostility towards the media and people see things on social media and just run with it, always thinking the media are the bad guys.

We can't pick and choose what the news is, and neither can the public. So long as the public watches the news, we will keep covering it. If I'm at a bomb alert or a murder scene and someone asks me genuinely if I had a choice where would I rather be, it obviously wouldn't be there.

I have no regrets about my life and career. I would do it all again the same way, I wouldn't change anything. The job I do defines me, it builds character. When I come home after work I chat with my wife and the kids about what happened that day and I suppose it's a way of getting it out, decompressing almost. It puts the day in context and then I get on with family life. I find that helpful. On my day off I won't look at news at all, I need a break from it.

I still hear their screams in my nightmares

Martin Dillon

MARTIN DILLON is an Irish author, journalist, and broadcaster. He has won international acclaim for his investigative reporting and non-fiction works on the Northern Ireland conflict

> *"I always wakened from this nightmare, shouting a final warning to the victims. Sometimes, I would sit up in bed, soaked in sweat. My nightmares worried my wife, but I never described the nature of them."*

Standing over a tortured body is a horror that never leaves you, especially when the victim is a 32-year-old man with learning difficulties. A cross and a number were burned into his back and his feet and hands were scorched. The number signified that he was not the first victim of his killers' grisly handiwork. The cross spoke to a perverse belief that God was on their side. The weapons used to create this horror were a red-hot poker pulled from a fire, or possibly a carpenter's torch ideal for stripping paint from wood, or flesh from bone. The torturers were members of the Ulster Defence Association who were determined to bring terror to the Catholic community in Belfast in 1972. The killers had plenty of time to make him suffer. They tortured him for hours before dumping his body. He had no intelligence about his own community to offer his killers, but they would not have believed him. I imagined hearing his screams for mercy in my nightmares. The killers finally put him out of his misery by firing two bullets into his skull.

The victim was Patrick Benstead, and I had the misfortune of standing over his corpse one early morning in an east Belfast alley. Cops at the scene mistook me for a forensic staffer and permitted me access to the body. This was a time when some of the most grisly killings of the Troubles were committed by both sides. The RUC had a policy of denying that killers were torturing victims and dismissed my report on the brutality of this murder. The majority of similar sadistic killings were the work of Protestant loyalist organisations.

I often wondered what it was like when killers looked into the eyes of victims they had marked for death. I found an answer years later when I raised this with Brendan Hughes, the late IRA intelligence chief. He was a major source of mine when I was writing *The Dirty War*. He helped me understand how IRA counter-intelligence functioned, and he told me what no other journalist knew – that the IRA held secret burials of those who later became known as 'The Disappeared'.

One evening while we were drinking in a Dublin pub, I found the courage to ask him what it was like to look into the eyes of a person sentenced to death after being interrogated by people under his command. He replied that it was like "staring into the recesses of a dark cupboard". As he said those words, it struck me that there was nothing but darkness in such a place. The revelation was precise and terrifying, yet fascinating in a macabre way. It is something I have kept confined to the recesses of my own thoughts all the years since.

I was reluctant to convey it to paper. There is something innately shocking and scary in the words and imagery. Perhaps, I feared giving it prominence in my own thoughts if I wrote it down. Did he find himself staring into such a dark space as his own life closed out, I have asked myself. He was living alone in Divis Flats, drinking heavily while dying of cancer. The man, whose counter-spying activities were legendary, even within Britain's MI5, was sad and disillusioned. He felt that the Republican Movement had betrayed the cause he had fought for.

I was a young reporter with the *Irish News* when bodies began appearing in alleys throughout Belfast, generally in the overnight hours. Subsequently, when I joined the *Belfast Telegraph*, there was no part of the city where I was not prepared to go to at any time.

I saw people who had been shot by the British Army and observed parts of bodies blown apart by IRA bombs, but I was anxious to find out why brutal killings like Patrick Benstead's were happening. I had begun building a personal file on what the media called sectarian murders when I was with the *Irish News*, and I continued adding to it when I joined the *Belfast Telegraph*. I was reporting with the *Telegraph* when Benstead was murdered. Shortly after his death, I learned from my police sources about a loyalist paramilitary phenomenon called 'rompering'. It involved killers taking their victims, mostly Catholic men, to illegal drinking clubs to beat and torture them in front of revellers.

My intense interest in the subject drew me into a close professional relationship with Denis Lehane, a colleague from the *Telegraph* newsroom. He was a journalist in training and arrived in the *Telegraph* newsroom with no experience in covering the conflict, as well as no contacts. I befriended him, as did my family, and I shared with him my interest in investigating sectarian murders. I showed him my files and we began working in our spare time on a series of articles about the growing use of torture. When we presented our findings to Eugene Wasson, the *Belfast Telegraph*'s editor, he rejected it. He doubted our claims about 'romper rooms' and suggested that we hand over the research to his features staff. We refused and undertook further research, which led to us to writing a Penguin Special edition – *Political Murder in Northern Ireland*. It was one of the first books to examine a major aspect of the Troubles. For students of the period, it still remains an important historical document.

In retrospect, my work as a reporter with the *Irish News* long before publishing this book provided me with material, contacts and the impetus to write later works like *The Shankill Butchers* and *The Dirty War*.

One man who oversaw the UDA during this period was Tommy Herron, the UDA's east Belfast chief. He was a wiry, fair-haired man in his early 30s with a violent temper. He had a Catholic heritage which he hid from his fellow UDA members. On one occasion, when I was interviewing him in his office at UDA HQ on the Newtownards Road, he pistol-whipped a young man who had dared question his order to extort money from a bookmaker. After the violent incident, Herron smiled as though he had just completed a brief work-out and resumed our interview. Afterwards, he asked me if I would like a drink, but I declined. He shook my hand as if we were buddies and expressed his hope that I would continue to print the truth about loyalists.

In September 1973, Herron who was always armed, was lured to his death by an unknown female. He accompanied her to a car later found abandoned outside Belfast. He was dead inside the vehicle with a single gunshot to the head. The assassination had all the hallmarks of a professional hit.

That violent period from 1969 through 1972/73 subjected me, and other reporters who spent a lot of time on Belfast's streets, to high stress levels. In retrospect, society as a whole was suffering a dysfunctional breakdown. Doctors were prescribing massive quantities of tranquilisers to people who lived in districts ringed by barricades. Behind the barricades, paramilitaries were in total control. They ran illegal drinking clubs run which remained open for at least 16 hours daily. My friend, the late Peter McKenna, a reporter with the *Irish Independent* who broke the story of the abuse of boys in the Kincora Home in east Belfast, once remarked that reporters would not have managed to get through the early 70s without alcohol and a few packs of cigarettes a day. He was a chain smoker.

"The alcohol soothed the nerves and dulled the mind," he would later observe.

We were all guilty of abusing alcohol because it offered periods of relaxation when the Troubles seemed irrelevant. We may have convinced ourselves that our all our risky behaviours were a temporary aberration. Whenever we discussed our work, we did so as though everything we observed happened in a vacuum to which we only shared a tenuous connection.

When I later began working for the BBC, I observed how many of my colleagues exhibited the same high stress levels. It was not so much a consequence of staff spending time at the cutting edge of daily reporting on the streets, since many BBC journalists were desk bound. Nevertheless, the fact of the daily chaos in society generated a frenetic pace which sucked us all into it.

Most BBC employees working in the fast-paced news and current affairs departments were conscious of what was happening around them. I recall talking to Peter McKenna about my investigation into the 1972 murder of 48-year-old

Thomas Madden. Like Benstead, he was the victim of sadists. Even though he was stabbed 110 times, he died slowly of strangulation, having been strung up from a wooden beam in a garage lockup. I saw the photos of his corpse, and it was clear that someone with a knife, possibly a pocketknife, had worked on his body like a sculptor carving a piece of wood. No single wound was sufficient to kill him.

When I was investigating this murder, I was grateful to Peter for locating a woman who had heard a man's screams for mercy on the night Thomas Madden was murdered. We often talked about the killing as if the more we discussed it we would somehow solve it. Each time we revisited it, Peter would ask me to describe the knife wounds. Dr Robert Marshall, the brilliant pathologist who examined the body, told me that he believed a small knife had been used by one of the killers. Looking back, our fascination with the murder and similar killings was somewhat bizarre. We were like directors of an absurd play, rewriting the script each time we reviewed it. Peter would imagine the number of killers involved, while I would insist that our focus should be on the one I called the prime mover; the dominant torturer with the knife.

We were aware that it had been an assassination team because Madden's body was dumped over a metal gate into a shop doorway, requiring several people to lift it high in the air before tossing it over the gate. These frequent exchanges between the two of us more often than not occurred when we were drinking.

I had nightmares during the early 70s, but I dismissed them while Peter laughingly insisted that he always slept soundly. I was not inclined to believe him, knowing that he drank a lot at the time and rarely went to bed sober.

Macabre images dominated my thoughts and my reporting in this period. I remember seeing many hooded bodies. It was the practice of the IRA and loyalist killers to place a hood over the head of a victim and tie it at the neck. I speculated that someone in each community had been delegated by terror bosses to sew pieces of pillowcases dyed-black to make hoods. It struck me that the killers used hoods not so much as signature items but to hide the twisted, tortured features of their victims as they transported them alive or dead from derelict homes, or from drinking clubs, to alleys, or to waste ground.

I once saw a British Army bomb disposal team attaching a rope to a hooded body off Cliftonpark Avenue in north Belfast. The body, with the hood still in place, was dragged along the street to ensure that it was not booby-trapped. It resembled a large garbage bag, and yet I knew it was a battered victim inside it.

Newspapers referred to the sites where killers left bodies as dumping grounds. Glencairn in west Belfast was such a place and was used by UDA/UVF killers from the Shankill district. Dark, shabby back alleys, known in the vernacular as 'entries', appeared to best suit the needs of killers on both sides. Ironically, killers never travelled far from their own homes or clubs to dispose of bodies. In retrospect, I believe the use of the media phrase, 'dumping grounds', for places bodies were found, reflected a subliminal recognition by journalists that killers considered their victims to be garbage. In my opinion, killers unconsciously used hoods as a way of further dehumanising victims.

Often, killers I interviewed exhibited a cold detachment. I realised that they surely presented as terrifying, nightmarish individuals when victims were in their hands. I remember a particularly vicious killer showing me a gun he insisted was "a real work of art".

One of my valuable sources was the late Dr Jack Nabney, a psychiatrist who was fascinated by murders I investigated. His intense interest in the subject sprang from the fact that some of his patients were among the victims from killing sprees in 1972/73. According to him, his patients, mostly young men, lacked the ability to understand the dangers of a tribal climate in which a wrong word or phrase was enough to lead a mentally challenged person into the clutches of sectarian killers.

In the 1980s, after he was semi-retired, we shared some fascinating conversations about the impact of the Troubles on all of us. He declared that there had been no studies devoted to the lasting psychological effects of violence on children who were silent witnesses to a raging war. Equally, no one had probed the results of violence on the paramilitaries themselves. He theorised that in decades to come society would discover threads of the psychological damage caused by the conflict if underlying emotional issues were not addressed. One of the startling events, which no one questioned because it happened without any fanfare, was the closure of a psychiatric unit in County Down designed to treat aggressive psychopaths. When I subsequently investigated this, I was informed that it had closed because of a lack of patients. The explanation answered some of my own concerns about that fact that there were many aggressive psychopaths in paramilitary ranks. In normal times, these men might have been shunned by society and possibly placed in psychiatric care, or admired because they tried to kick someone to death on the way from a football game.

In a dysfunctional society in the middle of a tribal conflict extremely violent men found acceptance. Their bizarre, erratic behaviour was not considered outside the norms of their environment. The closure of the psychiatric unit meant that men who were potentially a danger to society were on the streets and in terrorist organisations.

Since Dr Nabney lost patients to the conflict, he would often ask me to describe the personalities and motivations of killers I met, and to outline in detail the precise nature of some murders they committed. He admitted that he felt guilty about the murder of his patients even though he could not have changed the trajectory of their lives unless he had locked them away permanently from society.

He was especially keen on me opening up about my personal reactions to what I had witnessed. I resisted, convinced it would serve no purpose. In reality, I was subconsciously reluctant to open the door to my inner thoughts and feelings, fearing perhaps that reliving some of the horrors I had seen would be much too painful. He did not press me. Instead, he offered me a final piece of advice to me before I left Northern Ireland: "You can't hide from this, Martin, but it will find you in your quieter moments and when you are most vulnerable…in your sleep."

He was right. Nowadays, I tend to see a trigger for my nightmares, as time I began research for my books, *The Shankill Butchers* and *The Dirty War*. Investigating the Butchers murders forced me to delve deep into the grisly aspects of the early 70s killings in an effort to find links between the terror of that period and the Shankill Butchers.

My friend, the late Jimmy Nesbitt, the detective who brought many of the Butchers to justice, helped me grasp the minutiae of their crimes. He gave me access to the horrific photographs of the victims and provided insights into his pursuit of the killers, which became for him a personal crusade. We formed a close friendship, and I am sure he saved my life on several occasions by alerting me to terrorist threats. On one occasion, when I was due to fly into Belfast, he warned me about some chatter in loyalist ranks in Belfast about a plan to kill me. He also advised me to avoid certain areas after a police source overheard associates of the Shankill Butchers discussing how to kidnap me and slit my throat. It was Jimmy who frequently reminded me to examine my car in the mornings before driving to work in case an explosive device had been attached to its underside. His concern for me was not just about the danger I faced from loyalists but also from rogue elements in the IRA's ranks.

Our long conversations focused on each Butchers killing and how it had taken place. Consequently, I learned the identities of some of the most sadistic members of the Butchers gang whom Jimmy had been unable to bring to justice because their associates were too frightened to give evidence against them.

It was scary being in possession of such information, especially during the period I was writing *The Shankill Butchers – A Case Study of Mass Murder*. Since I could not legally name prominent Shankill Butchers without legal repercussions, I made it clear that I knew who they were. Instead of using their real names in the pages of my book, I used letters of the alphabet to identify them, starting with Mr A who is still alive at the time of me writing this piece. He was, however, number two in the gang hierarchy, though he was considered at times to be the boss. I described the crimes and respective roles of all those to whom I attributed letters of the alphabet.

Until Mr B died in a car accident in west Belfast, I could not reveal to the reading public that he was Lenny Murphy's brother John. On the day he died in August 1998, I received a phone call from my friend, the investigate author and journalist, Hugh Jordan, who asked me if I could confirm that John Murphy was Mr B, and I did so. It was somewhat ironic that John Murphy, who had a pathological hatred of Catholics, was comforted by a local Catholic man as he lay dying on Grosvenor Road.

After my book on the Butchers was published, threats to my safety intensified, and so too did my recurring nightmares about the Butchers murders. Interestingly, while I had been threatened by dangerous people and was forced more than once to stare down the barrel of a gun, those threats did not dominate my dreams. Instead, my nightmares were filled with sadistic killers and their grisly handiwork.

The person I turned to for advice regarding my stresses was Jimmy Nesbitt. He had an endearing smile and jokingly greeted me as "young man" each time we met. He reminded me of Raymond Chandler's morally reputable fictional detective, Philip Marlowe.

Like Marlowe, he was tall and thin; a chain smoker who led a very stressful life. He and his staff had more than 100 unsolved murders in their files. He spent long hours chasing down leads, examining tortured bodies in dark alleys, and interrogating dangerous men.

As he rose higher in the ranks of the RUC, he was tasked to supervise the security and re-location of supergrasses; terrorists who had given evidence in court against their former comrades. He was secretly appointed by MI5 to the role of negotiator in the event of terrorist kidnappings. Some people in Special Branch were unhappy with his closeness to me, and a senior figure wanted to limit his access to intelligence. That recommendation was dismissed. Jimmy was honourable and would never have betrayed the RUC, though he had a genuine mistrust, and dislike for parts of the intelligence community. He believed that British intelligence 'outfits' like 14th Intelligence Company acted like cowboys.

After he retired, he remained attached to his former colleagues and was often sought out for advice by the top brass in the Police Service of Northern Ireland, and the Intelligence community. He also worked with me on cold cases that I undertook on behalf of the families of some victims.

When I told Jimmy about my nightmares, he admitted that he had some, too. He never told his wife about them because she had suffered enough distress over the years while he was under threat from the IRA and some loyalist paramilitary figures. He only opened up about our common experience during two long lunches, accompanied by several bottles of wine. The alcohol seemed to loosen his tongue because he was very guarded about personal issues.

One of my recurring nightmares which fascinated him was related to a Shankill Butchers murder we had talked about on several occasions. In fact, we examined together the forensic images of the victim. In my nightmare, I am running after the victim, 21-year-old Stephen McCann, as he strolls along Millfield in the centre of Belfast with his 17-year-old girlfriend by his side. I know the Butchers are waiting in the shadows to abduct Stephen.

Once they have Stephen in the back seat of their car they will run a knife across his neck, just enough to open up a wound, though not deep enough to cut off his air flow or kill him. It will only be the start of their sadistic torture. They will beat him with their fists and tell him they are the infamous Shankill Butchers. Later, they will drag him from their car and force him to kneel. One of them will shoot him through the head before cutting his throat back to the spine.

In my nightmare, I am determined to prevent this horrific murder. I begin running after Stephen and his girlfriend. When I reach out to grab one of them, I stumble backwards, collapsing on the sidewalk. I want to shout a warning, but words will not leave my mouth no matter how hard I try. Frustrated and angry with myself, I get back on my feet and set off in pursuit of the young couple, sometimes reducing the gap between us to mere inches. But the moment I think I have may have hold of Stephen I fall backwards again. My feelings of helplessness and pent-up anger are made worse because the couple never turn to face me. I always wakened from this nightmare, shouting a final warning to them. Sometimes, I would sit up in bed, soaked in sweat. My nightmares worried my wife, but I never described the nature of them even when she insisted on knowing.

In January 2011, I was interviewed by the fine journalist Neil McKay for a BBC Radio 4 series, *The Scoop*, dedicated to the work of well-known investigative journalists. I talked about my personal experiences and reactions to violence I had witnessed. For the first time, I recounted publicly this particular nightmare. In doing so, I realised how terrible it must have been for police personnel, soldiers and first responders during the decades of violence. It must have been awful too for detectives like Jimmy, for ambulance staff and pathologists, who dealt with the effects of the violence, and for lawyers who had to examine gory post-mortem photographs and reports. All of those who witnessed violence will take time to heal, though the families of the victims of terrorism demand our greater support and understanding.

Ours was a society which dismissed the need for psychological help for children and teenagers who suffered trauma. Journalists and detectives were, in my experience, reluctant to admit how much they were troubled by their experiences. While it would be easy to attribute their silence to bravado, I suspect it was more likely due to a reluctance to admit to being vulnerable.

Over decades, my nightmares subsided but never vanished. Often, an unsuspected event would trigger them like when I discussed at length some of my personal experiences.

My friend, the late Dr Conor Cruise O'Brien who wrote the foreword to my Shankill Butchers book once shared with me that he was glad he did not have to live with the horrors in the book. Another friend, the Hollywood star Ed Harris, admitted that he stopped reading the book at night. Jimmy Nesbitt who lived with the horrors of the conflict warned me that the "dead have a habit of reappearing".

I understand the sentiment. Once you have spent a great deal of time bringing the lives of victims into your own mental space, it can prove difficult to remove them from your memories and your dreams.

As Peter McKenna used to say: "The dead who enter our nightmares are insisting we should not forget them." He said this over drinks, but I sensed he believed it. In the early 70s, he liked to spend evenings in McGlades, a bar at the back of the *Belfast Telegraph* which was the haunt of many journalists and local politicians.

The leading nationalist politician Gerry Fitt loved holding court in McGlades. He was often accompanied by Senator Paddy Wilson, his friend and political confidante. One evening while Peter was drinking with Gerry Fitt, Paddy Wilson was in a corner of the bar with 29-year-old Irene Andrews. She was Protestant and was well known as a fine ballroom dancer.

Gerry Fitt, for reasons he never explained, was unhappy about Paddy's attachment to Irene. Perhaps he sensed danger in the friendship. On this evening, Paddy was oblivious to

Gerry's concerns, and in Peter's view alcohol dulled his sense of propriety and ultimately his judgment.

Gerry Fitt took Peter aside and asked him for a favour. Peter should go out of the bar, return in a minute and whisper in Paddy's ear that he had taken a call from the public phone outside the lounge. The call was from Paddy's wife asking him to come home. Peter delivered the bogus message, but Paddy brushed him aside. Later that evening, Paddy left the bar with Irene. They drove to the outskirts of Belfast; unaware Ulster Freedom Fighter assassins were tracking them.

One of the assassins was John White, who used the moniker 'Captain Black' each time he called the media to claim responsibility for UFF murders. On the night of 25 June 1973, he and his associates dragged Paddy Wilson and Irene Andrews out of their car.

White was Protestant and so was Irene, but their shared religion would not protect her. White hated the fact that she was with a Catholic Senator. She was made to watch while White and several other men subdued Paddy Wilson by beating him. Then White stabbed him 29 times and slit his throat. Afterwards, he turned his rage towards Irene. She was stabbed 19 times.

Gerry Fitt never quite got over the shock of the murder of his friend. Neither did Peter McKenna, who claimed the stress of the period and too much alcohol led to Paddy Wilson engaging in risky behaviour. Peter felt there was nothing anyone could have done to prevent the double murder, but he still regretted that he had not been in the bar on the fateful evening. He often thought about the horror and pain Paddy and Irene suffered.

The tragic death of the young journalist Lyra McKee, killed by a stray bullet at a flashpoint in Derry in April 2019, reminded me of Jim Campbell and Martin 'Marty' O'Hagan, two journalists who were targeted for assassination by loyalist killers. Jim was shot inside his Belfast home and survived, albeit with a bullet which remains lodged in his spine. He was a courageous reporter and editor of the *Sunday News* and *Sunday World* during the most violent periods of the Troubles. He paid a terrible price for exposing some of the most dangerous killers within loyalism.

Marty O'Hagan emulated Jim who was his boss for some years in *Sunday World*. I knew both of them well. In the late 1980s, Marty was abducted by the IRA in South Armagh and driven to a farmhouse over the border in the Irish Republic where he was held for several days and interrogated about his visit to South Armagh. He told his abductors that he was following up a story for Sunday World and was making inquiries on my behalf about the murder of Captain Robert Nairac. The IRA released him after they were satisfied he posed no threat to them. He drove back to Belfast and came straight to my place. I advised him to write a story for the *Sunday World* about his abduction. I argued it would be wise to expose the IRA publicly since its leadership was not keen on making an enemy of the media by killing journalists. They might order their South Armagh operatives to leave Marty alone. He took my advice.

Some journalists felt that Marty pushed the envelope of risk building sources among dangerous killers in the loyalist paramilitary world. He was on first name terms with notorious UVF, UDA and Loyalist Volunteer Force killers in the Newry/ Lurgan/Portadown areas and never shrank from writing stories exposing their crimes, often using a pseudonym to do so. It was indeed a dangerous form of investigative journalism.

Aside from Jim Campbell, Marty had more contacts in loyalist paramilitary groups than any of his contemporaries.

He came under so many credible threats that his *Sunday World* bosses persuaded him to relocate to Cork for three years. During his time away from the conflict, he remained anxious to get back to the maelstrom of Northern Ireland journalism.

A colleague of mine once suggested that Marty had "an uncontrollable urge to court danger". I disagreed. Marty was familiar with the dark world of paramilitarism and was driven to reflect it. I warned him several times about the risks he faced, and I have no doubt he was cautioned by his mentor, Jim Campbell.

During the Troubles, some of us investigative journalists were cavalier and even flippant on occasions about death threats, but deep down we realised at a certain point we could not afford to dismiss them.

After writing *The Dirty War* in which I revealed for the first time the truth that the IRA had been secretly killing and burying people it considered informers, I received a number of threats to my life. My secret burial revelations led to the phenomenon known as 'The Disappeared'. There were threats directed at me from loyalists, too, and from some fringe republicans. I was informed that some members of the IRA considered killing me after I wrote that Brendan 'Ruby' Davison, the IRA's commander in the Markets area of Belfast, was a British agent.

My exposure of him as a double agent came in the wake of his assassination by loyalists and his burial by the IRA as a hero. He was interred in the Provisional IRA's memorial plot in Milltown Cemetery, which meant the IRA could never admit he had betrayed them. It was easier for Provisional IRA leadership to tell its members that I was trying to destroy the reputation of a patriot. My fellow author, Hugh Jordan, found out about it from his sources and warned me my life was in danger. I later revealed that Davison was also a paedophile. He remains buried alongside other notable IRA dead who are considered heroes by the organisation.

Even nowadays, the IRA has refused to admit that Davison was a major British intelligence asset codenamed Agent Ascot, or that he was a paedophile who abused teenagers in the Markets district where, as IRA commander, he had total control.

By early 91, I was so concerned about my safety that I decided to leave Northern Ireland. I had reached the conclusion that walking with danger as I did, like many journalists, including Jim Campbell, Marty O'Hagan, Henry McDonald, Jim Cusack, Liam Clarke, Hugh Jordan and Jim McDowell, did not make me immune. It brought me closer to the edge and was extremely dangerous. Living with a loaded gun by my bed only heightened my family's fears.

On 11 September 2001, hours after I watched the Twin Towers of the World Trade Centre collapse, the phone rang in my New York apartment. It was Marty O'Hagan. He was anxious to know that I was safe. I said I was worried for my friend, former FBI chief John O'Neill, who was on his first day as head of security at the Twin Towers. Alas my fears for John were justified. His body was found under the rubble of the towers days later.

I still remember vividly remember my conversation with Marty and how I warned him about the dangers to his life. I repeated something I had said to him years earlier that he must never underestimate his enemies in the paramilitary world. He assured me that he had made his peace with fringe loyalists and that many of his old sources were either dead, in jail or retired. By fringe loyalists he meant the LVF – Loyalist Volunteer Force.

I once met the LVF's charismatic leader, Billy Wright, at one of his secret hideouts where his musings about walking with the Devil were unnerving. He assured me, however, that he was walking with God and the Bible during our conversation. He was a cold, calculating terrorist.

Jim Campbell and Marty were familiar with Billy Wright and his terror activities. They credited him with the moniker 'King Rat' in their news stories about his organisation. He had no love for their journalism, and especially for Marty's reports about drug running by his associates in the Lurgan-Portadown area.

Wright was assassinated in prison in December 1997. His death only fuelled a more intense hatred towards Marty among his followers and accomplices.

Two weeks after Marty's 9/11 call to me, he was shot dead by LVF assassins as he walked home from a Lurgan pub with his wife. He had been warned the LVF was tracking his movements. I believe that Marty has never been given the accolades he deserved for his courageous reporting. Most of our journalism fraternity never worked so close to the edge as he did and, therefore, did not appreciate the risks he took to write his stories. He was resented by some colleagues because of his nerve to expose a general tendency of some journalists to fill the pages of papers with information from official sources.

He paid a high price for his courage. He was a victim of the Troubles and ultimately a victim of a very dangerous profession.

Some of us who chased ambulances like he did, and those who still do, can honestly say: "There but for the grace of..."